BRIGHT NOTES

FATHERS AND SONS AND OTHER WORKS BY IVAN TURGENEV

Intelligent Education

Nashville, Tennessee

BRIGHT NOTES: Fathers and Sons and Other Works
www.BrightNotes.com

No part of this publication may be used or reproduced in any manner whatsoever without written permission, except in the case of brief quotations in critical articles and reviews. For permissions, contact Influence Publishers http://www.influencepublishers.com.

ISBN: 978-1-645425-16-8 (Paperback)
ISBN: 978-1-645425-17-5 (eBook)

Published in accordance with the U.S. Copyright Office Orphan Works and Mass Digitization report of the register of copyrights, June 2015.

Originally published by Monarch Press.
Jane Wexford, 1966
2020 Edition published by Influence Publishers.

Interior design by Lapiz Digital Services. Cover Design by Thinkpen Designs.

Printed in the United States of America.

Library of Congress Cataloging-in-Publication Data forthcoming.
Names: Intelligent Education
Title: BRIGHT NOTES: Fathers and Sons and Other Works
Subject: STU004000 STUDY AIDS / Book Notes

CONTENTS

1)	Introduction to Ivan Turgenev	1
2)	Fathers and Sons	13
3)	Textual Analysis	26
	Chapters 1 - 8	26
	Chapters 9 - 16	43
	Chapters 17 - 23	61
	Chapters 23 - 28	77
4)	A Sportsman's Sketches	87
5)	Rudin	88
6)	A Nest of Gentlefolk	89
7)	On The Eve	90
8)	Character Analyses	91
9)	Critical Commentary	96

10)	Essay Questions and Answers	99
11)	Bibliography	103

INTRODUCTION TO IVAN TURGENEV

FAMILY BACKGROUND

In this post-Freudian age, the story of Ivan Turgenev's childhood and adolescence sounds like a contrived textbook case demonstrating intolerable psychological stress and disorder. Turgenev's mother, Varvara Petrovna Lutovinova, was an extremely rich, extremely ugly and extremely disturbed woman. As a child she had been beaten and attacked by a drunken stepfather, spurned by a harsh and sadistic mother, and rigorously disciplined by a guardian uncle who sought to disinherit her.

At 26, Varvara Petrovna found herself mistress of several estates and several thousand serfs. These she ruled with an unquenchable brutality-deporting at whim, flogging on pretext, raging for pleasure. Three years after she entered into her inheritance, Varvara Petrovna met by chance a young neighbor, a cavalry officer named Sergey Turgenev. The officer's family was in "reduced circumstances" and, although he was 6 years younger than the ugly, rich spinster and loathed the sight of her, when Varvara let it be known that she was interested in marriage, Sergey Turgenev's father begged his son to marry her and save their estate. Obediently, but reluctantly, he did marry her on January 14, 1816. But Sergey Turgenev was never able to conceal his intense dislike for the brutal woman. She completely usurped the management of the estates, and he devoted himself to a string of mistresses (at least one of whom bore him an illegitimate child). Sergey Turgenev, a cold and unapproachable man, occasionally turned on a warm charm, only to turn it off without warning.

INFANCY

Late in 1816, Varvara Petrovna bore a son, Nicholas. Then, on October 28, 1818, Ivan Sergeyevitch was born on his mother's estate in Oryol. Four years later a third son, Sergey (who was to die before he reached manhood) was born.

Varvara Petrovna was as capricious and brutal with her children as she was with her servants. And since Sergey Turgenev was all but a stranger in the household, the children were victimized by their mother with no interference.

In 1822, when Ivan was 4, the entire family, with a vast retinue of servants, made a tour of Europe. In Berne, the young Ivan was just barely saved from falling into a bear pit, and for several days afterward he was dangerously, almost fatally, ill.

When the family returned to Russia the systematic brutalizing of children and servants by the power-mad Varvara continued unabated. Turgenev once told a friend: "There is nothing I can remember childhood by. I have not a single happy memory of it."

EDUCATION

Ivan's early education was conducted according to the aristocratic tradition by a string of German and French tutors, whose constant comings and goings made proper education impossible. In 1827, when Ivan was 9, the family moved to Moscow and the boys were placed in a prep school. Ivan, already afflicted with hypochondriac tendencies which were to plague him all his life, was mercilessly tormented by the other boys for his physical fears. Prep school lasted only a year and a half, and then, after trying other schools, intense private tutoring began as Ivan prepared for the Moscow University exams.

UNIVERSITY

In 1833, at the age of 15, Turgenev entered the university. But he lasted only one term there, falling ill with some undiagnosed disease. His father, who suffered extremely from gall stones, was also ill, and died the next year when Ivan was 16. In the fall of 1834, Ivan entered St. Petersburg University, a student in the "philological faculty."

Between 1834 and 1837, when he graduated from Petersburg, Turgenev spent his winters immersed in his studies and in the literary life of Petersburg. (He was already writing poetry and poetic narratives.) During the summers he went with his family to Spasskoye (his mother's favorite estate), and managed to maintain a not wholly miserable relationship with his tempestuous mother.

BERLIN

In the spring of 1837, Turgenev left for Berlin to complete his studies. The boat trip from Petersburg to Berlin was eventful. As the steamer neared the coast of Germany, it suddenly caught fire. According to all accounts, Turgenev lost his head, and some witnesses claimed he dashed about crying: "Save me, save me, I am my mother's only son." Forty-five years after the fire, Turgenev wrote a "reminiscence" called "A Fire at Sea" in which he admits to having been "perturbed" during the panic, but denies the withering accusations of his utter cowardice (the incident had been revived by his enemies).

Once safely in Berlin, Turgenev threw himself into the active intellectual life of the German "Hegelian idealists." But the "word" continued to emanate from his mother at Spasskoye, and in October, 1839, he was ordered to come home. He stayed at Spasskoye until January 1840, and then left for Italy.

IMPORTANT FRIENDSHIPS

In Rome, he re-met, and became intimate friends with, the gentle and brilliant philosopher Stankevich. Stankevich "breathed fire and strength into us" Turgenev was later to write. But by June of 1840, at 27, Stankevich was dead of consumption.

In July of the same year, Turgenev met the irrepressible future anarchist Mikhail Bakunin. Under Bakunin's tutelage, Turgenev became a rabid Hegelian romantic idealist, and the two young men became constant companions. Turgenev, back in Berlin, spent most of his time reading and studying and, as his biographer David Magarshack says: "It was there that he laid the foundation of that great accumulation of knowledge which made him the greatest European of his time."

RETURN TO RUSSIA

In 1841, Turgenev returned to Spasskoye, but finding life with his mother increasingly intolerable, he moved in the spring of 1842 to St. Petersburg where he studied for his M.A. He completed parts of it with distinction, but then abandoned the idea of obtaining his degree. His life was in a turmoil. First, one of his mother's seamstresses bore him a daughter (when Varvara Petrovna learned of the girl's pregnancy she drove her away and Turgenev settled her in a flat in Moscow). Second, Turgenev had become involved with Bakunin's sister, Tatyana, and the friendship was ending with great disenchantment. The bitterness over this relationship brought Turgenev's romantic Hegelian phase to a rapid end. He entered the civil service and prepared to work for the gradual emancipation of the peasants.

But at the same time he was writing poetry. One poem, Parasha, attracted the attention of the great literary critic Belinsky, who in 1843 lavishly praised the poem in print.

For the next few years Turgenev wrote prolifically. He resigned his post at the civil service, and, since his mother would not support a "pen pusher," he suddenly found himself humiliatingly poor.

PAULINE VIARDOT

In the winter of 1843, something happened to Turgenev which he described "as having had a most powerful influence on the whole of my life." He met a celebrated opera singer named Pauline Viardot. "From the very first moment I saw her I was entirely hers." Turgenev became this exotic woman's devoted and humiliated "slave." (Her husband, Louis Viardot, tolerated Turgenev's constant presence in his household and the three of them comprised an intermittent menage a trois until, 40 years later, Turgenev died in Pauline's house.) From what evidence there is, Pauline never returned Turgenev's passion and frequently treated him with icy indifference and hauteur, interspersed with periods of tenderness and submission.

In 1845, Turgenev traveled to France to be with Pauline, and on his return devoted himself solely to literature. He became friendly with all the important literary figures-Dostoevsky, Goncharov, Herzen, Grigorovich and others. And he began his series of "Sportsman's Sketches" which were to meet with great success.

A FULL-TIME WRITER

When the Viardots returned to Russia in 1847 for a concert tour, Turgenev joined them; when they left he left with them. He followed them around Europe, writing his sketches and articles and sending them to Russian publications. Turgenev was in France during the 1848 Revolution, and was greatly stirred by the tumult around him.

In June of 1850, he returned to Russia. He had, by then, completed his "Sportsman's Sketches" and several plays (including *A Month in the Country*, which was not performed in Russia until many years later). During his absence his mother had appealed to him to return, and when he refused, she stopped sending him money and, as further punishment, took his 7-year-old daughter from her mother and put the child to work in the kitchen. Shortly after Turgenev's return home, Varvara Petrovna died and Ivan was at last an independent and rich man.

GOGOL'S OBITUARY

During October 1851, Turgenev had his one and only meeting with the great Gogol. Four months later the master died.

Turgenev wrote a glowing obituary for the St. Petersburg News which the censor banned. The authorities, strained after the European events of 1848, wanted no public show of sympathy for the great satirical realist. Turgenev sent the obituary to Moscow where it appeared in the Moscow News. It was not an incendiary article, but one line got Turgenev into trouble: "He is dead, this man whom we have the right, the sorrowful right granted to us by his death, to call great."

Three days after the obituary was published, Turgenev was arrested for "manifest disobedience." He was kept in jail for a month, after which he was confined under police supervision to his estate at Spasskoye for sixteen months. During Turgenev's exile, *The Diary of a Sportsman* was published (containing twenty-one of the "Sportsman's Sketches"). The book was an instantaneous success.

LITERARY SUCCESSES

By 1854, Turgenev was back in St. Petersburg, leading an active and exciting literary life. Then, in 1855, he completed his first big work, Rudin. Published in 1856, Rudin was a great triumph for Turgenev. In the summer of that year, he returned to Paris and Pauline Viardot. Their relationship soon became tumultuous and Turgenev suffered nervous disorders akin to a breakdown. Despite his physical and mental disarray, Turgenev traveled around Europe, meeting the literary elite and turning out articles and stories.

In 1858, he finally returned to Russia and finished *A Nest of Gentlefolk*, an enormous and immediate success. With time out for a quick European jaunt, he set to work on *On the Eve* which was published, with hue and cry, in 1860. "The upper strata of Russian society were alarmed by Turgenev's novel," wrote a critic. On February 19, 1861, when Turgenev was in Europe, the manifesto emancipating the peasants was published in Russia. Turgenev returned to Spasskoye in May, 1861, to finish work on *Fathers and Sons*. During this summer he had a foolish, furious argument with Tolstoy which led to a challenge to a duel-fortunately the duel was never fought. Turgenev returned to Paris in September with the completed manuscript for *Fathers and Sons* in hand. When the storm of reaction broke over the novel (see below), Turgenev became utterly disillusioned with his native land, and from then on he was more or less an expatriate.

He lived for eight years in Baden-Baden, where Pauline Viardot had set up a singing school. He wrote only one novel during this time, the ill-received and bitter Smoke. But, during a brief visit to Russia in 1871, he was given an enthusiastic reception by his ever-growing audience.

YEARS IN FRANCE

After the Franco-Prussian War, Turgenev moved to Paris, where he spent the last 12 years of his life. He became involved with French literary circles although he never fully appreciated French literature: "Their literature stinks of literature," he wrote a friend, "that's what's so bad." He was talking about Zola, Daudet, de Maupassant, de Goncourt and even at times his dear friend Flaubert. Turgenev was regarded as a master at the famous French literary dinners of the 1870s, and his style was praised by all the great writers of the age.

Turgenev suffered violently from gout, but he continued to travel and write. In 1876, he finished his longest, and in ways most ambitious, novel, *Virgin Soil* which, when it was published in 1877, caused another storm of vituperation from left and right. Turgenev had expressed in this novel his still-held conviction that the Populist movement was premature and Russia would not be ready for her revolution for 30 years.

Once more, as after the failure of *Fathers and Sons*, Turgenev vowed never to write another thing. But in 1879, on a "business trip" to Russia, he was so widely and enthusiastically acclaimed, he forgot his vow of punitive silence.

LAST YEARS

Starting in 1878, Turgenev began writing his *Poems in Prose*, which contained his thoughts on philosophical, political and personal subjects. Some of them were published in Russia in 1882; the remainder were published posthumously.

Although Turgenev at times during his last years felt physically fit and optimistic, by May of 1882 he was bedridden by his "gout." The disease (actually cancer of the spinal cord) became debilitating, and Turgenev suffered cruelly. In July of 1883, he wrote his famous letter to Tolstoy, beseeching the younger man to return to literature (which he had abandoned in favor of a life of religious asceticism). After that, Turgenev could devote himself only to agonized dying. He died on September 3, 1883, and, after the writer Renan had delivered a commemorative service at the Paris train station, Turgenev's body was shipped to St. Petersburg where his funeral assumed the character of national mourning. "Turgenev," says his biographer Magarshack, "had come home to stay."

THE TIMES

Reformers

In the nineteenth century in Russia the great, continuous, ubiquitous struggle was for reform-reform of serfdom, of political persecution, of censorship; reform of autocracy, of oppressive social conditions; reform of conservative unenlightenment. When issues are so large, those who plan to solve them never agree on the ideal solution. Russian intellectuals fell into two vast opposing camps with many "battalions" in each.

Slavophiles

On one side were the admirers, adorers of Mother Russia. Russian culture, they insisted, should preserve its uniquely Slavic characteristics based on a religious-mystic inheritance from the past. These reformers, called Slavophiles, felt that Russia was betraying herself by accepting the corrupt traditions of the West - by imitating Western dress, fashion, literature and manners. Russians should rather dress in their national "costumes," use their native language, and work for change within the framework of Russian customs, folkways and institutions. (Victor Sitnikov, Bazarov's "disciple" in *Fathers and Sons*, is a caricature of the Slavophile.)

Westernizers

On the other side were the Westernizers - the reformers who favored European "enlightenment" and refinement and who claimed Turgenev's active and devoted sympathy from the time he was a schoolboy. Having grown up in surroundings which every day showed him the brutality of serfdom and the oppressiveness of autocracy, Turgenev had good reason to join the ranks of European and emigre reformers. Although he argued with nearly all his contemporaries at one time or another over his unshakable confirmation of the European way (Dostoevsky so despised his sympathies that he drew a searing portrait of Turgenev in *The Possessed*), Turgenev could see no hope for a Russia saddled with her ancient superstitions and unenlightened institutions. So strong were these convictions, and so despairing were his hopes for a modern Russia, that Turgenev spent the last 20 years of his life almost continually in Europe.

"Commitments"

Although he has been called the most European of Russian writers, Turgenev never wrote of anything but his native land. His artistic approach and style may have appealed to his European contemporaries, but his preoccupations were with Russia's present and future. If Turgenev's indictments of the "backward giant" sound mild to modern ears, we must keep in mind the terrible, strict censorship imposed on all speech and writing by a serfdom terrified by the European events of 1848.

Turgenev became a master of criticism by implication. He managed to sound noncommittal, to appear highly objective, while in fact conveying a great commitment.

But his political commitment was never so overpowering as to obliterate his art. He was frequently accused during his lifetime of having no philosophy, of changing his opinion with each change of the prevailing political wind. He was not a Populist or a Slavophile; not a conservative or a believer in an imminent revolution; he publicly opposed violence but fervently believed in reform; he had no religion. Everyone at one time or another had a grievance against him. Turgenev was not sure of the solutions and he occasionally sided with one idealist or another, always casually, never permanently. Turgenev was not a political philosopher; he was a writer. As Edmund Wilson notes: "He sticks to his objective judgment, his line of realistic criticism, his resolve to stand free of movements, to rise above personalities, to recognize all points of view that have any sincerity or dignity, to show Russia how to know herself."

Literary Life

Turgenev knew or met nearly every literary "giant" in the giant-populated mid-nineteenth century. Although he is eclipsed today, at least in non-Russian circles, by his more famous contemporaries Dostoevsky and Tolstoy (Dostoevsky was three years younger, Tolstoy ten) his reputation both at home and in Europe during his own lifetime was enormous.

Perhaps because he lived in Europe, perhaps because his style had the European touch, Turgenev was the first of the great Russian writers to win a European reputation. Pushkin was barely known on the Continent, Lermentov and Gogol merely names, but Turgenev, during his own lifetime, was translated into French, German and English, and he himself was the adopted Slavic darling of the French literary circles. When he died in 1883, a London journal noted: "Europe has unanimously conferred upon Turgenev the first place in modern literature."

Although the West now turns to "weightier" writers for its impressions of nineteenth-century Russia, twentieth-century Russians read Turgenev's tales, sketches and novels with the same avidity and delight that Westerners did a century ago.

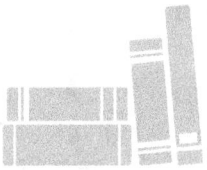

FATHERS AND SONS

INTRODUCTION

In August of 1860, Turgenev wrote to a friend: "I have thought of a subject for a novel, I wonder what will become of it?" For a long time Turgenev had given thought to a new kind of man, zealous and materialistic, that he observed in increasing numbers among the young generation of reformers. He feared, however, that perhaps he was running after a "phantom" in trying to record this new man and postponed time and again putting these observations on paper. Then, one day early in August 1860, he was walking on the beach and the writer suddenly saw in his mind a picture of a dying man. This man became Bazarov and in time the characters surrounding him took shape.

In July, 1861, Turgenev finished *Fathers and Sons*, noting in his diary his fear that readers "will not believe that all the time I was writing my novel I felt an involuntary attraction to [Bazarov]."

When he returned to Paris (from Spasskoye where he had spent the summer) Turgenev read his new novel to his friends. They were unimpressed by it, and the author began a series of extensive alterations. He toyed with the possibilities of delaying publication in deference to the political turmoil at home, but his

Russian publisher insisted "that he must have the goods" (as Turgenev wrote to Dostoevsky) and so in March, 1862, *Fathers and Sons* appeared in the monthly, *The Russian Herald*.

Though he was prepared for a storm of reaction from some political circles, Turgenev never dreamed of the avalanche of abuse which was to descend upon him. Before the storm, there was a pleasurable calm during which Dostoevsky wrote an enthusiastic letter to Turgenev voicing his complete sympathy and understanding of the book and its hero. "Now I am no longer worried about my novel; it has done what I intended it to do," Turgenev wrote. He spoke too soon.

Critics of every political persuasion poured abuse and insult upon him. Conservatives condemned his portraits of the useless older generation. Radicals accused him of sneering at the younger generation. The younger generation deplored the "caricature" he had drawn of them in Bazarov. Alexander Herzen wrote from his self-exile in London that Turgenev had "wanted to put in a word in favor of the fathers" but instead of "giving the son a good hiding he has flogged the fathers." The Russian police did not agree: "Turgenev has branded our adolescent revolutionaries with the caustic name of nihilists and shaken the doctrine of materialism," they recorded.

Turgenev was shaken and confused by the misinterpretation of Bazarov by the young generation of reformers. In a long letter dated in April, 1862, to Konstantin Sluchevski, a young liberal, Turgenev defended and explained his feelings about Bazarov. Far from holding Bazarov up for ridicule and then killing him off before he could accomplish anything, Turgenev saw the young nihilist as "honest, truthful, and a democrat to the marrow of his bones." He had hoped to show "the idleness of the elegant and noble gentry," not praise it. "My entire story," he insisted, "is directed against the gentry as the leading class."

Perhaps part of Turgenev's failure to make his point unequivocally lay in his great emotional ties to Nikolai Petrovitch and the "old" generation. "Nikolai Petrovitch is myself ... and thousands of others.... They are the best of the gentry, and that is just why I have chosen them to show its insolvency."

On the subject of Bazarov and his attractiveness Turgenev was vehement: "If the reader does not love Bazarov in all his coarseness, heartlessness, pitiless dryness, and causticity ... the fault is mine and I have not attained my goal." Turgenev was not willing to "sugar-coat" Bazarov to make him immediately appealing to the younger generation he so eagerly courted. "I was dreaming of a gloomy, savage and large-scale figure half sprung from the soul, strong, malicious, honest - and for all that condemned to perish because he stands at the threshold of the future."

Turgenev had undertaken to present a favorable portrait riddled with defacing pockmarks. From the outcry it would seem that only the blemishes came through.

In June of 1862, Turgenev returned to St. Petersburg. By chance he returned on the same day that a huge fire, allegedly set by the St. Petersburg students, was raging. "When I came back to Petersburg," he wrote, "on the very day of the ... fire - the word 'nihilist' had been caught up ... and the first exclamation that greeted me from the first acquaintance I met was, 'Look what your nihilists are doing! They are burning down St. Petersburg!'" Worse than this, Turgenev's old political friends were cold and indignant to him while enemies from the conservative camp offered congratulatory kisses.

From all over Russia, Turgenev received abuse on the one hand for being a die-hard reactionary and on the other for pandering to the nihilists and "groveling at the feet of Bazarov."

OBJECTIVE OBSERVATION

The fantastic **irony** of this tumultuous reception, which caused a stir "unprecedented in the literary history of Russia," is that *Fathers and Sons* is not a political tract at all. Turgenev had long been fascinated by the young generation of reformers, the "men of the sixties," but felt that he, "a man of the forties," could not fully understand them. As one contemporary critic put it: "Turgenev ... turns to the young generation and asks it: "What kind of people are you? I don't understand you.... But this is what I observed about you-explain to me.'"

More as a novelist than as a politician Turgenev sought to clarify this new man. He waited many years before writing his book until he could find a living, human model-a "living person in whom the various elements were harmonized together." Finally, during his travels in England, he met a young Russian doctor whose intelligence and uncompromising personality greatly impressed him - and it is this doctor, he later revealed, who served as a model for Bazarov. The iconoclastic nihilist is not a lifeless composite of ideas and principles but the study of a very compelling personality.

Turgenev's books are, after all, about people not thoughts. The great force of *Fathers and Sons* lies not in its theoretical philosophies, or even in its detailed and accurate depiction of Russian society in the 1860s. It lies in its sympathetic and sensitive characterization and in its revelation of the great forces of life: love, death, conflict, nature.

The critic Nikolay Andreyev asserts that love is the central **theme** of the novel: "Bazarov who set out to overthrow all the false values of the fathers is eventually spiritually broken by love." Pavel's life founders on love. Love is the cause of Nikolai's regeneration. Arkady gives up his pretensions for love. Bazarov, struggling against the great love of his parents, loses his vitality. And surely, the exploration the "love" between Bazarov and Anna is a fascinating focus for the book.

If love and love relationships (friends for each other, parents for their children) are the central **theme** of the book, there are several other important ones. There is the timeless, ageless conflict between the generations which is so delicately, so carefully drawn, that its truth strikes home at this very moment. The scenes between Bazarov and his doting parents bring a blush of recognized truth to every reader who has rebelled against parental authority.

Death, too, although it comes at the end of the book, is central to the work's meaning. In 1859, Turgenev wrote to a friend: "we are all condemned to die. Can there be anything more tragic than that?" And he later admitted that Bazarov's death seemed so tragic to him that as he wrote the last pages "I had to turn my head so that my tears would not fall on the manuscript."

Bazarov is senselessly cut down before he has accomplished anything, before anyone except those who love him have heard or understood him. The only comfort we have for this sad death comes at the very end of the book when Turgenev gives us hope that Bazarov's ideas will someday be reconciled to an indifferent world.

AS SOCIAL HISTORY

It is not antithetical to posit that while *Fathers and Sons* is about characters, about the great struggles of life, it also records social history and looks to the future. Almost as though fulfilling a prophecy, the Bazarov type did come to the fore and nihilism was all the rage for a while in the university circles. Turgenev once observed that Russia would not be ready for its "Bazarovs" for several decades in the future. He was right. Forty-three years after *Fathers and Sons* was published came the great struggle of 1905, and in 1917 the successful revolution which destroyed the old and introduced the new materialism was fought.

The social climate in which Bazarov lived (and failed) is characterized in sensitive touches. The novel gives us a panoramic view of the "backward giant" shackled by obsolete ideas, manners, customs and, of course, serfdom. Turgenev makes no effort to conceal his contempt for the Russia which cannot receive Bazarov. The peasants are dishonest, uncomprehending and devitalized by their long oppression. The aristocracy is mannered, effete, "dead." The new intellectuals are phony, shallow and ultimately disinterested in action. The well-meaning reformers of twenty years ago are ineffectual and cautious. Government officials are stupid, self-impressed and mindless. It is not a heartening picture that Turgenev paints, and it is no wonder that, with the novel's unenlightened reception, he chose for himself a life of exile from the land on whose horizon he could see little light.

STYLE

For the modern reader, accustomed to a realistic style in which the author's presence is nowhere felt, *Fathers and Sons* will seem old-fashioned and contrived. Turgenev makes no effort to conceal himself as omniscient author. He intrudes with observations of his own, interrupts the narrative for necessary bits of information and biography, and lumps together exposition with no regard for the natural revelation of background material. The opening chapter is so hopelessly uncontemporary for a generation suckled on Joyce, Henry James, Proust and Faulkner as to be discouraging. And the neat wrapping of the package in the final chapter, in which the characters take a formal bow, seems dreadfully contrived.

But for all its old-fashionedness, *Fathers and Sons* is a masterpiece of simplicity and economy. Turgenev conveys Bazarov's great urgency and the intensity of his conflicts with little sensationalism. With serene objectivity Turgenev dramatizes the major issues of an age: atheism vs. orthodoxy; science vs. faith; autocracy vs. democracy; tradition vs. revolution, and yet he defines these major conflicts within a small compact frame.

Turgenev's forte lies in illuminating great **themes** by the use of small, intimate detail. Look, for example, at Chapter XX in which Bazarov returns home. How much we learn of the old Bazarovs and their way of life, their relationship to their son, their hopeless out-datedness, from such little homely details as a new silk handkerchief, a surreptitious blessing, a servant's new boots and a reconverted "bath house." Henry James once said of Turgenev's style: "It [has] the beauty ... of the finest presentation of the familiar."

STRUCTURE

Fathers and Sons is divided into seven distinct sections - the sections marked off by geography rather than **theme**. The first four sections are expository: at Maryino; at the town of X-; at Nikolskoe; at old Bazarov's. The last three sections wrap up matters in sequence at the three important places: Maryino, Nikolskoe and old Bazarov's. The tacked-on epilogue is not germane to the novel's structure.

The structure is startlingly clean and direct. When business is concluded in one place we move on to the next. There are no overlaps of time; the story unfolds in simple, direct chronological order over a period of a few summer months.

THEMES

The novel is as unified thematically as it is schematically. We are always dealing with Bazarov and his reactions to or effect upon different characters and environments. Each character is observed in relation to Bazarov: How do they measure up to him? How do they respond to him? How do they contrast with him? As Bazarov travels from place to place we see the responses he evokes and learn of his impressions and reactions. We are exploring the character of Bazarov primarily and the nature of the people around him.

Around and through the intimate pictures of his characters, Turgenev reconstructs a world charged with conflict. The primary conflict, of course, is the ageless struggle between fathers and sons. Implicit in this conflict are disagreements about the great social and political **themes** of the time: emancipation, philosophical idealism, orthodoxy, Westernization, education.

Standing apart from these social problems is the question of nature's indifferent majesty. Turgenev sometimes steps back from his characters to revel in the beauty which surrounds them. He relates nature to his characters and plot by rather transparent links which merely give him an excuse to expand on one of his favorite (and most skillfully executed) **themes** - the awesomeness and beauty of the Russian land.

RUSSIAN NAMES

Readers unfamiliar with the Russian system of nomenclature may find the multitude of names allotted to each character somewhat confusing. Generally, a Russian male has three names; his first name, his patronymic (his father's name) and his last name: Thus we might have an imaginary character named Alexander Nikolaevitch Chukovsky (Alexander, son of Nikolai Chukovsky). He might be referred to in any of the following ways:

Surname alone: Chukovsky

First name and surname: Alexander Chukovsky

First name and patronymic: Alexander Nikolaevitch

First name and abbreviated: Alexander Nikolaitch

Patronymic: Abbreviated patronymic alone: Nikolaitch

First name alone: Alexander

French form of first name: Alexandre

Affectionate nicknames: Shura, Shurochka, Sashka, Sasha, Sashenka, etc.

The name problem is further complicated by disagreement among translators. Alexander may be transliterated as Alexsandr; Nikolai may appear as Nicholas, Nikolay; Nicholay; Chukovsky may look like Tchuhovsky, Chukoffsky, Tchukovsky, or Chuhoffsky.

To add to the confusion, women have their own, feminine endings. Thus Alexander's wife would be Sonia Andreevna Chukovskaya (Sonia, daughter of Andrey, wife of Chukovsky). Alexander's daughter would be Maria Alexandrovna Chukovskaya (Maria, daughter of Alexander Chukovsky). Some translators, in the interest of simplicity, omit these endings (Constance Garnett is among them). Thus we may find Anna Sergyevna Odintsova referred to as Mme. Odintsov, or Anna Odintsov.

It is worth a few moments before reading a Russian work to get each of the characters straight and to review the names by which they might be designated.

IMPORTANT CHARACTERS IN THE NOVEL

Yevgeny Vassilyitch Bazarov: A young medical student with "nihilistic" views. Called Yevgeny by his friends, Enyusha by his mother.

Vassily Ivanovitch Bazarov: Bazarov's father, a retired army doctor.

Arina Vlasyevna Bazarov (A): Bazarov's mother. Called Arisha by her husband.

Anna Sergyevna Odintsov (A): A rich and beautiful student, Bazarov's friend. His family calls him Arkasha.

Nikolai Petrovitch Kirsanov: Arkady's father, a provincial landowner.

Pavel Petrovitch Kirsanov: Nikolai's brother (Arkady's uncle), an aristocratic dandy.

Fenitchka: Nikolai Kirsanov's mistress. Formally addressed as Fedosya Nikolaevna.

Anna Sergyevna Odintsov (A): A rich and beautiful widow.

Katya: Anna's younger sister. Formally addressed as Katerina Sergyevna.

BRIEF SUMMARY

In the spring of 1859, two young friends return home to the provinces of Russia from their studies at the University of St. Petersburg. Their first stop is Maryino, the "estate" of Nikolai Petrovitch Kirsanov, the father of the younger of the friends- Arkady Kirsanov. Nikolai, a widower, lives on his failing farm with his defeated, elegant, effete brother Pavel, and his young, innocent mistress Fenitchka. Arkady and his friend and mentor, Yevgeny Bazarov, clash with the older men on matters of philosophy and principle. Bazarov, a passionate "nihilist" (from the Latin nihil, meaning nothing), believes that everything must be destroyed before a new world can be built. He devotes himself to scientific and medical study, and facts are the only matters of importance to him. Arkady, although devoted to his family, proudly defends Bazarov and his new ideas.

After a few weeks the friends leave Maryino for a brief visit to the neighboring town of X-. There they meet foolish officials and even more foolish "emancipated" liberals. They also meet Anna Sergyevna Odintsov, a very rich young widow from the country. Arkady is immediately fascinated by her, and Bazarov too finds her physically and intellectually exciting. She invites them to come visit her in the country, and in a few days they travel to her estate, Nikolskoe.

Both young men are intrigued by the self-possessed Anna; but as she treats Arkady like a younger brother, he turns for companionship to Anna's young, reticent sister Katya. Bazarov's passions are intolerably aroused by the icily captivating Anna and, after two weeks, in a burst of feeling, he declares his love for her. She repulses him. Furious with his own "romantic lapse" and her heartless playing with him, he leaves the next day for his family's home. Arkady goes with him.

Bazarov's old parents cannot hide their overflowing joy at his return after an absence of three years. But young Bazarov, stung by his recent rejection and infuriated by his parents' sentimental fussing over him, leaves without warning in three days.

After a brief and unrewarding stop at Mme. Odintsov's, the young men return to the Kirsanov estate at Maryino. Bazarov devotes himself slavishly to his studies, and he and Arkady's uncle Pavel (who are ardent antagonists about theories and manners) carefully avoid the searing arguments of the first visit. After ten days, Arkady grows intolerably restless and impulsively gallops off to Nikolskoe where he pleasantly resumes his growing relationship with young Katya and begins to lose his passion for Anna.

At Maryino, meanwhile, Bazarov has begun to take great pleasure in his friendship with the young and wholly honest provincial girl Fenitchka (Nikolai Kirsanov's mistress). One day in the garden Bazarov kisses Fenitchka, and they are seen by Pavel, who himself has been nursing a passion for the young girl.

With Ludicrous formality, Pavel challenges Bazarov to a duel with pistols. When they fight the next morning, Bazarov, without taking aim, shoots Pavel in the thigh. Pavel, after several weeks in bed, recovers. But while he is ill he is tended by Fenitchka who mortally fears him. In a searching "examination" he convinces himself that the Fenitchka-Bazarov kiss in the garden was innocent on her part, and that she truly loves Nikolai. Pavel begs his brother to do the honorable thing and marry Fenitchka - an act which Nikolai has been delaying in deference to his brother's aristocratic feelings of propriety and class distinctions.

Bazarov leaves Maryino the day after the duel and goes to Nikolskoe to tell Arkady what has happened. While he is there, he makes an uneasy peace with Anna and says a final good-bye to his ex-disciple Arkady, who has proposed to the lovely young Katya.

Bazarov returns to his parents' house, but after a few days' work grows restless and listless. He begins to help his old father in his medical practice. One day, while performing an autopsy on a peasant who has died of typhus, he cuts his finger. Within a few days he is in a raging fever, and after one last, moving interview with Anna, he dies.

Six months after Bazarov's death, Arkady marries Katya, Nikolai marries Fenitchka, and Pavel leaves for Moscow. The Kirsanovs, father and son, stay at Maryino and finally put it in order. Anna eventually marries an "icy" intellectual, and Bazarov's old parents weep mournfully over his tangled grave.

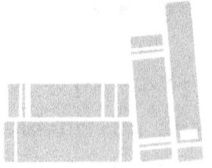

FATHERS AND SONS

TEXTUAL ANALYSIS

CHAPTERS 1 - 8

CHAPTER I

The opening chapter is an introduction to one of the "fathers," Nikolai Petrovitch Kirsanov. Kirsanov is waiting at a posting station near his provincial property for a carriage to arrive from St. Petersburg. His son, Arkady, is returning home from the city having just completed his degree, and Kirsanov is restless with anticipation and excitement. Turgenev gives us a formal biographical introduction to the father.

Kirsanov is "a little over forty" and he waits hatless and in dusty clothes at the posting station. Twelve miles from the station is his farm of 5,000 acres with 200 peasants working it. Kirsanov's father had been a Russian general, coarse but not cruel. His mother had doted on the material benefits of being a general's wife, and had little to do with Nikolai and his older brother Pavel. Kirsanov was educated at home by inadequate tutors until he was 14. Later, his father planned for him to join the Army, but on the day the news of his commission arrived, Nikolai broke a leg. Disappointed, the General gave up hopes of his son's military career, and brought him, when he was 18, to St. Petersburg University to earn his degree. Nikolai lived there in an apartment with his brother Pavel until he graduated in 1835. His father died (having been forced to retire after an unsuccessful review) and his mother soon followed the General to the grave. Nikolai, as soon as mourning was over, married his landlord's daughter with whom he was madly in love. The two were blissfully happy and after a while they settled in the country and their son Arkady was born.

For ten years they lived in perfect harmony, and then suddenly, in 1847, Kirsanov's wife died. Broken and distracted, Kirsanov finally managed to "lose" himself in the management of his land, and in 1855 he in his turn brought his son to the university in St. Petersburg. For three winters Kirsanov lived with his son in the city, but this year, 1859, his land had demanded his attention and he had remained in the provinces. Thus he waits impatiently on a May morning for his son's return.

When the carriage arrives, Kirsanov embraces the young graduate with a surge of love and delight.

Comment

Turgenev is very careful in this first chapter to set the time of his narrative. He scrupulously dates the important milestones in Kirsanov's life: the year he graduated from the university was 1835; his wife died in 1847; he brought his son to the university in 1855, and the day he waits at the station is May 20, 1859. These are clearly the important dates in Kirsanov's uneventful life, and, by carefully recording them, Turgenev makes us feel we have a sense of the man.

As we meet him, Kirsanov is "already completely gray-headed, plump and slightly stooping." His life has been far from remarkable or eventful and the death of his beloved wife has left him melancholy and lonely.

Although Kirsanov has partitioned his estate among his peasantry (more than two years in advance of the 1861 emancipation) his farm has not been successful. His clothing is dusty, his servant is insolent. He is not the affluent country gentleman. Our sympathies immediately go out to the waiting father who watches, surrounded by a pullet, a "dirt bespattered cat" and a plump pigeon, for his son's carriage to come into sight. His thrill as he catches sight "of the band of a student's cap" is touching and we have already begun to care about him.

CHAPTER II

Kirsanov is slightly embarrassed and a little timid at the reunion. His excitement leaves him nervous and fussy. Arkady is gay and responsive and eager to introduce his father to his "great friend" Bazarov, who has come with him from St. Petersburg and has promised to stay with them for a while.

Kirsanov is delighted to meet one of his son's university friends. He quickly goes to shake Bazarov's "ungloved red hand" and, although Bazarov hesitates, he finally meets the handshake. We are given a few fleeting impressions of the visitor. He wears a "long, loose, rough coat with tassels," his voice is "lazy but manly" and he appears self-confident and intelligent. To Kirsanov's pleasantry, "I hope ... you won't be dull with us," Bazarov moves his lips "just perceptibly but makes no reply."

As the trio prepares for the trip to Kirsanov's house, Arkady and his father climb into the family carriage and Bazarov returns to the coach in which the students have traveled from St. Petersburg. As the driver harnesses fresh horses, Bazarov calls to him familiarly, "Come, hurry up, bushy beard!" And with everyone settled, the vehicles more away from the station.

Comment

Kirsanov's little fussiness and formalities are the telltale signs of his generation. He immediately asks Bazarov his formal name ("your name and your father's") and he fidgets about the carriage having only two seats, fretting that Bazarov will have to ride in the less comfortable coach.

Arkady reassures his father: "You must not stand on ceremony with him, please. He's a splendid fellow, so simple- you will see."

Kirsanov's servant, Piotr, with his turquoise earring and plastered hair, is definitely a man of modernity. He is so modernized that he merely bows to the young master from the distance and does not rush to kiss his hand.

Through little actions the generations are already confronting each other. Even the civilities of reunion are tinged with conflictive overtones.

CHAPTER III

On the trip home, Arkady shows his boyish delight at his homecoming, but at the same time he tries to avoid any sentimental display. His father tells the boy about the difficulties he is having on the farm (called Maryino). The peasants refuse to pay their rent, and they neither work hard nor use their tools skillfully. Kirsanov has dismissed his freed serfs from positions of responsibility and now has a townsman as bailiff on his property.

While discussing the changes at Maryino, Kirsanov confesses to his son, with great embarrassment, that a girl, Fenitchka, is now living with him. Arkady takes the news light-heartedly and "reveling in a consciousness of his own advanced and emancipated condition" assures his father there is no cause for shame.

As they approach Maryino, Arkady's delight in the spring day, the fresh country air, briefly fades as he opens his eyes to the rundown property. They pass "low hovels under dark and often tumble-down roofs." They see neglected, peeling and dilapidated buildings. The peasants they meet are in tatters, their animals half-starved. "Reforms are absolutely necessary," thinks Arkady, "... but how is one to begin?"

The green brightness of the day quickly restore Arkady to his good spirits and, as he turns to his father with affection, Kirsanov quotes to him a sentimental passage from the poet Pushkin. Although Arkady hears him with sympathy, the two are interrupted by a yell from Bazarov for a match. Arkady passes one back to Bazarov's coach, and he in turn quickly lights up a smelly cigar Bazarov has passed forward to him. Kirsanov, never a smoker, "was forced to turn away his head, as imperceptibly as he could for fear of wounding his son." In a short while they reach Maryino, or "as the peasants had nicknamed it, Poverty Farm."

Comment

We begin to have a feeling in this chapter of the time and venue of our tale. By describing the short trip to Maryino, Turgenev provides himself with the opportunity of surveying, through Arkady's eyes, the condition of the countryside. And it is a poor condition indeed.

The peasants they pass are ill-clad; their hovels are dirty and neglected. The animals are near starvation, and the trees are broken and stripped. Although under the spring sunshine the countryside is at its best, Arkady can imagine the sight during the cold, barren winter.

The exchange between Arkady and his father about Kirsanov's mistress is painful. They speak in French so that Piotr, the servant-driver, will not understand them. (In pre-Revolution Russia the gentry were educated in two or three foreign languages. Whenever they wished to hide their meaning from servants or peasants they spoke among themselves in French.) Kirsanov is ashamed of his mistress because of her youth, because of her class and because of her compromising situation, and he is most ashamed to have to discuss the matter with his son. Arkady tries to show his father how liberal and emancipated he is by reassuring him there is no need to apologize. And yet, the young man is acutely embarrassed by the discussion.

As the father turns to discussions of their future together working the farm, Arkady tries to change the subject. And when Kirsanov begins to quote poetry, the antithesis of the hard-headedness Arkady has been learning from Bazarov, Bazarov interrupts their sentimentality with his cheap black cigar. It is a little matter, this interruption, but a forewarning of larger more significant interruptions to come.

CHAPTER IV

This chapter serves as an introduction to the members of Kirsanov's household. When Bazarov, Arkady and Kirsanov alight at Maryino, they are met, not by a crowd of house serfs, but by one little girl, Dunyasha, and a young, stylishly dressed lad (Pavel Kirsanov's servant).

As soon as they enter the house, Bazarov sprawls carelessly on a sofa and announces he is hungry. Kirsanov's old servant, Prokofitch, comes to greet Arkady, kisses the young master's hand and retreats with servility from the room.

A moment later, Kirsanov's older brother, Arkady's uncle, Pavel Petrovitch, enters. His dress and behavior are in keeping with the latest European styles and "his exquisite hand with its long tapering pink nails" is set off by a snowy white cuff secured by a single, big opal. Pavel is perfumed and groomed and highly mannered. He takes an immediate dislike to Bazarov and asks later of his brother if that "unkempt creature" is to stay with them.

Supper on this first evening is strained and awkward and, when it is over, Bazarov comments to Arkady: "Your uncle's a queer fish... Only fancy such style in the country! His nails, his nails - you ought to send them to an exhibition!"

Arkady defends both his uncle and his father from Bazarov's attacks: he is happy to be home, and while he knows his family is far from perfect and does not meet the demands of his exacting friend, he is content to be sleeping in his own bed surrounded by the loves of his childhood. While Arkady sleeps, his father daydreams agitatedly by candlelight and his uncle sits up by the dying fire involved in rambling thoughts. In a small back room the girl Fenitchka dozes and listens to the regular breathing of her sleeping baby in the next room.

Comment

The battle lines are drawn at this very first encounter. Bazarov says very little but he and Pavel instantly mistrust each other. Bazarov's dress and manners are rough and contemptuous. When Pavel offers the young man his hand in greeting, Bazarov refuses to shake it. When Kirsanov suggests that Bazarov might like to see his room before supper, the newcomer tosses out: "No, thanks; I don't care about it."

But Bazarov is not wholly in the wrong. Pavel's dress and manner are, in fact, terribly affected for country living. He appears indeed "an antique survival." As for Kirsanov, Bazarov thinks him a "good-hearted fellow" who "doesn't know much about farming." The student's judgment of Kirsanov was verified by the conditions he saw on the drive from the posting station.

As for Arkady, he listens in agreement to his friend, but his pleasure at being home and his delight at being surrounded by the people and objects he loves far outweigh his newly learned sophistication.

The closing paragraph, a description of the dozing Fenitchka attending her baby, comes as a jolting shock. We suddenly understand Kirsanov's reluctance and embarrassment on the subject of his mistress. We are meant, in the tradition of old-fashioned story-telling, to anticipate with suspense and curiosity the young men's discovery of the illegitimate child.

CHAPTER V

The next morning, Bazarov is the first to awake in the household and, after surveying the unimpressive "manor house" and grounds, persuades two young farm boys to join him in a walk to a nearby swamp where he seeks frogs for his medical experiments.

In his absence, Kirsanov and Arkady sit down to morning tea, attended by the young girl Dunyasha, not by Fenitchka who has sent word that she is ill. With great embarrassment Arkady leads the discussion around to the young mistress. "She has no need to be ashamed ... could I be willing to hamper your life ... in the least thing?" Arkady, though unsteady, takes great pleasure in delivering a "lecture" to his father about his own enlightened views. Kirsanov is still greatly embarrassed, but when Arkady jumps up with the intention of paying Fenitchka a visit, his father does not stop him.

Kirsanov is confused about the wisest way to handle his son and his own relationship to his mistress. Perhaps Arkady would have respected him more if he had hidden his embarrassment and made no apologies. But when Arkady returns he is full of affection: "Why didn't you tell me I had a brother? I should have kissed him last night, as I have kissed him just now." Father and son embrace with relief and affection. Their sentimental rejoicing is interrupted by Pavel who immediately asks after Arkady's "new friend." Bazarov is a medical student, Arkady explains, and he is visiting them on a stopover before he goes to his father's house sixty-four miles away. Bazarov's father, it turns out, has been a surgeon in Arkady's grandfather's regiment.

"Well, and what is Mr. Bazarov himself?" asks Pavel pointedly. "He's a nihilist," answers Arkady promptly. "A nihilist is a man who does not bow down before any authority, who does not take any principle on faith, whatever reverence that principle may be enshrined in." Arkady's relatives are unconvinced. "Well, I see it's not in our line. We are old-fashioned people," retorts Pavel cynically.

Fenitchka interrupts the exchange and with great confusion and embarrassment she attends to the tea. When she leaves, Bazarov returns, all muddied, from the swamp. "He has no faith in principles, but he has faith in frogs," mutters Pavel. But sensing this is no time for a confrontation they change the topic to the problems of managing the farm.

Comment

This first morning on the farm plunges us directly into the **themes** of the book. Bazarov, on his way to hunt frogs for his scientific experiments, immediately makes friends with the farm boys. He "possessed the special faculty of inspiring confidence in people of a lower class, though he never tried to win them." This is the human, redeeming side of Bazarov, much to be admired, which we are likely to lose sight of as he treads roughly over the Kirsanovs.

The difficulty Arkady and his father have in discussing Fenitchka gives the older man an insight into "the inevitable strangeness of the future relations between him and his son."

And when Pavel starts right in on his criticism of Bazarov, Arkady is put in the position of "defender of the faith" against his uncle's attacks.

Neither Pavel nor Kirsanov has much interest or confidence in Bazarov's nihilistic views. "There used to be Hegelists, and now there are nihilists," chides Pavel ironically. But in deference to Arkady, who is compassionate and loving with his family, the brothers suspend their attack. They lightheartedly scoff at the views Arkady has shared with them, but they do not yet feel greatly threatened.

CHAPTER VI

When Bazarov has put away his frogs, he comes back and joins the family at tea. He and Pavel immediately antagonize each other. Pavel's "aristocratic nature was revolted by Bazarov's absolute nonchalance." He resents the abruptness with which "this surgeon's son" answers his questions.

Bazarov explains his belief in scientific fact and discovery but his acceptance of no scientific theory or authority. "They tell me the truth, I agree, that's all." As they speak of recent German experiments, Pavel reveals his prejudice against Germans:

"Russian Germans I am not speaking of now; we all know what sort of creatures they are. But even German Germans are not to my liking." Pavel allows that Schiller and Goethe might be worth something, but Bazarov cuts him off: "A good chemist is twenty times as useful as any poet," he pontificates.

The jousting becomes more heated and finally, in response to Pavel's barbed inquiries, Bazarov asks: "What's this, an examination?" Kirsanov, conscious of his duties as host, interrupts the exchange and consolingly asks Bazarov for his expert scientific help in running the farm. "I am at your service, Nikolai Petrovitch," he retorts, "but ... one has first to learn the a b c, and then begin to read, and we haven't set eyes on the alphabet yet."

When the two older men leave to attend to farm matters, Arkady chides his friend for his rudeness to his uncle. "You have hurt his feelings," accuses Arkady. "Well, am I going to consider them, these provincial aristocrats! Why, it's all vanity, dandy habits, fatuity," is Bazarov's reply.

Comment

The gulf between the generations appears from this scene to be wholly unbridgeable. Bazarov's arrogant glib pronouncements are as odious to the genteel brothers as their "decadence" is to him. Bazarov is a breed of intellectual they have never seen before. He is prepared to tear down all the existing principles and methods in favor of scientific "fact" but he has no plan for rebuilding or replacing. Destruction of the existing is his password.

The brothers, for their part, have struggled to keep informed of latest advances within the existing social structure and can feel nothing but contempt for the young man who would antiquate them.

The unfortunate Arkady is caught between the two. While he reveres Bazarov's intellect and sympathizes with his views, he loves his family and would pity his uncle, not ridicule him. Pavel's prejudices and snobberies are far from admirable - he dislikes all Germans and sneers at a lowly "surgeon's son" - but Bazarov's rudeness and insensitivity balance out this snobbery.

CHAPTER VII

In defense of his uncle and in an attempt to evoke Bazarov's sympathy, Arkady tells his friend his uncle's "story." Turgenev breaks the realistic style in a direct address to the reader: "And Arkady told him his uncle's story. The reader will find it in the following chapter."

Pavel Petrovitch Kirsanov was, like his brother, educated first at home and then in the cadet corps. He was always exceedingly handsome and self-confident. As a young man he was a great success in society and even his affectations were attractive. Women adored him; men envied him. At 28, he was a captain in the Army, looking forward to a brilliant career.

Then he met, in St. Petersburg, a neurotic, unhappy eccentric Princess who despised her tepid husband and entered eagerly into adulterous affairs. Pavel fell madly in love with the enigmatic lady and, although she gave herself to him, she remained somehow aloof and mysterious. Her unpredictable moods tortured him while she loved him "but when she grew cold to him, and that happened rather quickly, he almost went out of his mind." The Princess went abroad to escape Pavel's attentions. Ignoring all advice, he resigned his commission and pursued her. For four years he chased around foreign lands following her at times, avoiding her at times. For one month, after four years, she took him back as a lover, but after that she steadily avoided him.

Pavel returned to Russia, but he could not resume his old life and wandered about like a man possessed. He "no longer expected anything much of himself or of others, and he undertook nothing." Ten years passed by "colorless and fruitless," and then one day he heard that the Princess had died in Paris near insanity.

The same year Nikolai Petrovitch's wife had died and the brothers decided after some time to live together at Maryino. Pavel spent his time reading English literature and copying the English style of life and dress-but always in isolation. He maintained his affectations even in the country: he was perfumed, well dressed, a gourmet and incorruptibly honest. The neighbors considered him "stuck up" but admirably aristocratic.

Bazarov is unimpressed with the tale. He scorns Pavel for staking his whole life "on one card." The obsessive love Pavel had for the Princess "that's all romantic, nonsensical esthetic rot. We had much better go and look at the beetle."

Comment

Pavel Petrovitch's story is a strange and sad tale. Although he threw away his life for a foolish fantasy, there is something compelling and moving about his self-destruction. Clearly his suffering was extreme and his obsession consuming. Bazarov protests that a fellow who "lets himself go till he's fit for nothing, is not a man, but a male." For all his suffering, it is true, Pavel has learned neither humility nor tolerance. He still "imagines himself a superior creature," insults Bazarov and cultivates his "aristocratic manners" while the lower classes starve around him.

In defense, Arkady observes: "But remember his education, the age in which he grew up." "Every man must educate himself," decrees Bazarov. Although it comes from the rude iconoclast, clearly Turgenev agrees with this decree. Background is no excuse for blindness. And yet, Pavel's history is told with empathy and compassion. We are meant to pity the unhappy aristocrat. But Bazarov's brash contempt for the "tragedy" is not altogether unreasonable. Progress was never made by defeated country aristocrats.

CHAPTER VIII

While Arkady tells Bazarov about his uncle, the two older men interview the bailiff, a hired townsman. The estate, which had "recently been put on to the new reformed system," was not running at all smoothly. The bailiff accuses the peasants of drunkenness and thievery, and Nikolai Petrovitch has exhausted both his own and his brother's funds. Pavel loses interest in the interview and leaves his brother and the bailiff in the study. He goes instead to Fenitchka's room on the pretext of asking her to order him some green tea from the town.

The two "relatives" are very ill at ease with each other. Fenitchka fears Pavel, who has scarcely ever spoken to her, and she is greatly embarrassed by her position in the household. On an impulse, Pavel asks to see the baby Mitya. Fenitchka goes into the nursery to fetch the child, and Pavel, surveying her room, is touched by its simplicity and hominess. When the baby is brought out, Pavel and Fenitchka try desperately to cover their awkwardness in conversation about the infant. The interview is interrupted by Kirsanov who is delighted at the unaccustomed attention his brother is paying to his child. Pavel, inexplicably uncomfortable, hastily retreats.

Once again Turgenev interrupts the narrative with some necessary **exposition**. "Nikolai Petrovitch had made Fenitchka's acquaintance in the following manner. He had once happened three years before to stay a night at an inn in a remote district town." The woman who kept the inn was an extremely pleasant and efficient widow and Nikolai Petrovitch asked her to be his housekeeper. She consented and within a few weeks she arrived at Maryino with her 17-year-old daughter Fenitchka. About a year later Fenitchka got a spark from the stove in her eye and Kirsanov treated it. He was greatly moved by his contact with the young girl, and with time they became comfortable with one another. When Fenitchka's mother died suddenly "she was so young, so alone. Nikolai Petrovitch was himself so good and considerate... It's needless to relate the rest..."

Kirsanov stayed a while playing with his baby while Pavel returned to his study and, throwing himself on the sofa, stared at the ceiling "with a face almost of despair."

Comment

By showing the contrast between the two brothers' relationship to the simple Fenitchka, Turgenev throws into relief the differences between them. The older generation is by no means homogeneous. Nikolai's affair with Fenitchka is tender, unaffected and filled with love. He is greatly moved by the girl's serenity and is anxious to protect and please her. Their relationship, far from being scandalous, is pure and moving.

Pavel frightens Fenitchka and challenges her. She feels she must dress up her baby before he is brought to Pavel, and she herself must put her hair in order in his presence. Pavel, by inference, and perhaps from jealousy, disparages their relationship by insinuation. "He's like my brother," he observes. "Yes ... there's an unmistakable likeness." The implication is that Pavel had suspected the child might have had some other father.

Fenitchka's simplicity and fidelity depress Pavel as he compares his brother's good luck in love to his own great misfortune. Pavel would be incapable of selflessly loving the artless young girl.

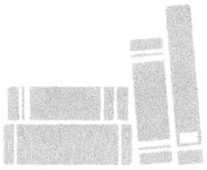

FATHERS AND SONS

TEXTUAL ANALYSIS

CHAPTERS 9 - 16

CHAPTER IX

On the same day that Pavel visits Fenitchka, Bazarov meets the girl for the first time. While he and Arkady are walking in the garden, they come upon Fenitchka in an arbor. After learning from Arkady who the pretty young woman is, Bazarov approaches her and comments on the healthy look of her baby. At his request, Fenitchka gives Bazarov the infant to hold, and to her amazement he makes no protest at being handled by a stranger. "Children are always good with me ... I have a way with them," states Bazarov.

Arkady, eager to please Fenitchka, asks to hold the child also. But this time the baby throws back his head and screams, much to his mother's dismay.

As they continue on their walk, the two friends discuss Fenitchka's position. "I think [my father] ought to marry her," comments Arkady. "You still attach significance to marriage; I did not expect that of you," chides Bazarov. But in a few moments they change the subject. Bazarov tells Arkady of the dreadful condition he has found the estate to be in. "The cattle are inferior, the horses are broken down ... the workmen look confirmed loafers... and the dear good peasants are taking your father in to a dead certainty." From the farm they get on to nature, and Bazarov denigrates Arkady's romanticizing of the natural beauties around them: "Nature's not a temple, but a workshop, and man's the workman in it." Just as Bazarov is being his most unsentimental, nihilistic self, the sound of a 'cello reaches them. Nikolai is practicing with gusto a Schubert sonata. Bazarov bursts into laughter at the "absurdity" of the head of the household in an isolated district playing his 'cello for pleasure. Arkady does not support Bazarov's laughter with so much as a smile.

Comment

The complexity of Bazarov's character is shown by the antithetical incidents which open and close the chapter. With Mitya, Fenitchka's infant, he is loving, relaxed, responsive and successful. He takes time to praise the mother and child and pass a pleasantry with the silly girl Dunyasha. The brash young nihilist does indeed seem to have "a way with children." And, yet, the same young man can cruelly laugh at and deride Nikolai before his adoring son. Bazarov can be very cruel (as when he accuses Arkady of wishing to be rid of Fenitchka so he needn't share his inheritance with Mitya). But there is something open and spontaneous in his nature which attracts to him the simple, innocent and unaffected.

CHAPTER X

For two weeks life goes on at Maryino in a comfortable routine. Bazarov with his rudeness, carelessness and hard work has established himself in the household. He and Fenitchka have become very much at home with each other, while Nikolai vaguely fears his influence on Arkady and yet respects his intellect and research. The servants and farm hands are delighted with any scrap of attention he pays to them. Only Pavel and the old servant Prokofitch are offended by and displeased with the insinuating visitor.

One day, a Arkady and Bazarov talk in the garden they are overheard by Nikolai. "Your father's a nice chap ... but he's behind the times; his day is done," counsels Bazarov. Arkady makes no answer, and his father steals away unnoticed. When Nikolai tells his brother of the overheard conversation, Pavel's smoldering anger bursts into flame: "I hate that doctor fellow; in my opinion, he's simply a quack." Nikolai is not so vehement. He regrets that he has been "left behind" and can no longer communicated intimately with Arkady. But he admits that "Bazarov is clever, and knows his subject."

That same day, at evening tea, the "tussle" that Pavel has been spoiling for finally comes about. It starts out on the subject of man's personal dignity which Bazarov ridicules: "You respect yourself, and sit with your hands folded; what sort of benefit does that do to the bien public?" At this jibe Pavel turns white with anger. "What is good for something according to you?" Bazarov dismisses logic, principles, rules and authorities. "At the present time, negation is the most beneficial of all - and we deny ... everything!" Construction is not our business now, asserts

Bazarov, "the ground wants clearing first." Pavel protests that the denigration of tradition and faith goes against the Russian people. "But am I not Russian, too?" asks Bazarov. "Ask any one of your peasants which of us - you or me - he'd more rapidly acknowledge as a fellow-countryman. You don't even know how to talk to them."

Pavel attempts to weaken Bazarov's stand by pointing to all the unsuccessful "reformers" of the past. Bazarov corrects him: "We advocate nothing," he declares. Having seen the ineffectiveness of incessant talk about reform, the nihilists "decided not to undertake anything," to, as Pavel puts it, "confine [themselves] to abuse."

As the argument waxes, Pavel's fury mounts. Arkady proudly goes to Bazarov's defense while Nikolai attempts to make peace. Finally, Bazarov, in an attempt to end the discussion, says: "I shall be quite ready to agree with you ... when you bring forward a single institution in our present mode of life, in family or in social life, which does not call for complete and unqualified destruction." Pavel lamely mentions the family and the communes, both of which Bazarov shows to be corrupt and disintegrating.

The two young men walk off, and the heart-sore Nikolai turns to his brother and tells him an anecdote. "I once had a dispute with our poor mother; she stormed and wouldn't listen to me. At last I said to her, "Of course, you can't understand me; we belong,' I said, 'to two different generations.' She was dreadfully offended, while I thought. 'There's no help for it. It's a bitter pill but she has to swallow it.'" Nikolai is prepared to swallow his pill in turn, but his brother still believes in their own generation's rectitude.

Comment

The core of Bazarov's philosophy-or anti-philosophy-is carefully spelled out in this conflict-charged chapter. As a nihilist he is out to destroy the existing forms, and only after the ground is cleared of stultifying conditions can a program evolve. Nothing has meaning-not talk, not theory, not principle-until man has freed himself of his restrictive and ineffectual traditions.

As unpleasant and disrespectful as his manner might be, there is something compelling in Bazarov's arguments. The old reforms have not succeeded, the time-honored traditions have decayed and foundered. Adherence to the old rules has occasioned no improvement.

The tension in the chapter comes not so much from the conflicting theories as from the embattled personalities. We cannot sympathize with Bazarov's attack on the vulnerable Pavel, and we grieve for Nikolai's alienation from his son. And yet Pavel's haughty "refinement" and Nikolai's bumbling ineptitude deprive them of our full sympathy. Turgenev skillfully manipulates our emotions back and forth between the antagonists, now calling forth our scorn for Bazarov's rudeness, now our sympathy for his "revolt."

Arkady emerges during the argument as a faithful if not fully informed disciple. He readily sides with his friend against his family, but he does so with such innocence and such childlike pride that we are inclined to smile at his sincere efforts to be a convincing nihilist.

Nikolai's willingness to accept his own "old-fashionedness" despite his great efforts to keep abreast and be "modern" is testimony to his liberality, generosity and compassion. He is anxious for the love and respect of his son, and in his eagerness to please he is willing to step aside. Nikolai may be old-fashioned in his methods, but Turgenev is at pains to display his gentle humanity, which must ultimately endure and prevail.

CHAPTER XI

Having aroused our tenderness for the gentle Nikolai, Turgenev goes on, in the following chapter, to give us further insight into his loneliness and despair. After the discouraging "tussle," Nikolai goes to his favorite arbor in the garden. Overcome by melancholy, he muses about the ever-widening gap between his son and himself. Although he feels he is closer to the truth than the young people, he senses that they have "some superiority over us ... Doesn't their superiority consist in there being fewer traces of the slave owner in them than in us?"

But even as he thinks these despondent thoughts, he looks about him at the natural splendors of the garden at evening and feels sure all this beauty is not to be denied.

As the peace of the arbor settles on him, he begins to dream of his adored wife. He longs to feel her near him. At that very moment Fenitchka interrupts him, bringing him back to the reality of his age and situation. Unable at the moment to relinquish his "enchanted world" he dismisses Fenitchka gently: "I'm coming, run along." And then he thinks: "There it is, the traces of the slave owner."

Grown restless with the force of his emotions, he walks about the garden, melancholy and filled with yearning. He begins to cry-aware of the sentimentality of "a man of forty-four years old, an agriculturist and a farmer" shedding causeless tears.

The mood is interrupted by Pavel who moves away after a few moments to become absorbed in his own thoughts.

In the meantime, Bazarov and Arkady decide to leave Maryino and go the next day to visit a minor dignitary, a relation of Arkady's who is visiting a neighboring town. After spending a few days in the town, Bazarov will go on to visit his own father: "I've not seen him for a long while, and my mother too; I must cheer the old people up."

The next day they are off - to the relief of the old people at Maryino and the regret of the young.

Comment

The quietness of this chapter is a dramatic change from the tumult of the preceding one. It is the aftermath of the storm. Nikolai's sad revelation that he can never escape the onus of his generation - the decadence of slave-owning - and his great yearning for his dead wife are filled with sorrowful emotion. The magnificence of the garden in evening with the peasant on horseback riding by provides a perfectly integrated setting for Nikolai's great melancholy. His memories of his wife are charming, graceful and filled with pleasure. And yet that peasant, with the patch on his shoulder, cannot be forgotten. Something must be done for him-but this romantic, dreaming in his garden, does not seem to be the man capable of making the great effort necessary for it.

At the same time, the tough nihilist Bazarov shows a surprising sentimentality. He is, after all, not wholly heartless. In deciding to go to visit his parents he allows: "They've been good to me, especially my father; he's awfully funny. I'm their only one too."

With the young people's departure the first section of the novel concludes. One pair of fathers and sons have confronted each other with mutual distress. A distress, it is true, tempered by love, but nonetheless an unsettling dissonance between generations.

CHAPTER XII

The town of X - which the young friends go to visit is in political upheaval. The young governor "at once a progressive and a despot" has quarreled with every faction of the town and the ministry at St. Petersburg has sent a commissioned authority to investigate the tumult. This "authority" is Matvy Ilyitch Kolyazin, a distant cousin of Arkady's. Matvy is portrayed by Turgenev in searing terms. He wears a star [medal] "on each side of his breast-one, to be sure, a foreign star not of the first magnitude." This Matvy is extremely vain, but his manner, at first blush, is so open and affable that "he might even be taken for 'a jolly good fellow.'" And yet, in important matters he wields authority with a heavy hand, although he is easily taken in by "any moderately experienced official." Although he tries to present himself as au courant in literature and politics he really has only a few presentable facts at his command. "He was an adroit courtier, a great hypocrite, and nothing more ... but he knew how to manage his own business successfully."

Matvy receives his cousin Arkady good-naturedly and advises the young man to call on the Governor, particularly since that official is giving a ball in Matvy's honor two days hence. Accordingly, Arkady and Bazarov visit the Governor who is "in an everlasting fuss and hurry." He invites the young men to his ball and, as they leave his office, they meet on the street an old friend of Bazarov's in Slavic national dress. This friend, Sitnikov, has come to X - with his father on business and has been excited to learn that Bazarov was in town. Sitnikov, a self-styled "disciple" of Bazarov's, convinces the friends to join him for lunch at the house of an emancipated lady friend of his, Mme. Kukshin. He lures them with the promise that she will offer them champagne.

Comment

With the introduction of a new section, Turgenev also introduces a new tone. In his description of the town functionaries he is a removed observer and his note is cynical and ridiculing. We find none of the sympathy for Matvy, the Governor or Sitnikov that we had for the members of Kirsanov's household. Matvy, who "had not long passed forty," is revealed as an ineffectual poseur, given to petty vanities and needless exercise of power. He is a scathing caricature of the middling official on the way up in the bureaucratic hierarchy. With "no special aptitude for affairs, and no intellect," his main concern is for his own advancement. Matvy is a thoroughly unlikable, uninspired bore, one of the many of his kind running the machinery of his country.

The Governor is no better. Although affable, his lack of organization keeps him forever in a bustle. "In the morning he used to put on a tight uniform and an excessively stiff cravat," and when Arkady and Bazarov call on him he gets confused and regards them as brothers, calling both "Kisarov." Hardly the prototype of the capable and efficient administrator.

But it is not only the men of success who come in for ridicule. Sitnikov, a disciple of the "new," is nothing so much as a fool. His Slavic national dress, finished off by "over-elegant gloves," is a **parody**. He pretentiously flatters Bazarov: "I am indebted to him for my regeneration." And his enthusiasm is unreflective: "Would you believe it ... when Yevgeny Vassilyitch [Bazarov] for the first time said before me that it was not right to accept any authorities. I felt such enthusiasm ... as though my eyes were opened."

Sitnikov is the son of a rich liquor man, and obviously not a great favorite of Bazarov's. When Sitnikov promises there will be champagne at his friend's house, Bazarov asks him what he will promise with. "With my own head," answers Sitnikov. "Your father's purse would be better," mocks Bazarov. Here is a trait of Bazarov's we haven't seen before, a quick humor, taunting perhaps, but clever. We are meant here to applaud it; another intimation that, despite what his critics said, Turgenev really did like Bazarov.

CHAPTER XIII

Sitnikov's lady friend, Avdotya Nikitishna, is a rollicking, shrill, boring, emancipated "bohemian." Separated from her husband, she leads what she considers to be a totally free life. Her house and her person are rumpled and in disarray. She prattles endlessly about the latest theories and about the emancipation of women. Sitnikov proudly seconds her empty liberal pronouncements, while Bazarov mocks them both and works on the champagne.

Amid Avdotya's pointless chatter, Bazarov asks if there are any pretty women in the town. Avdotya tells him of her friend

Mme. Odintsov, a clever rich widow who, Sitnikov adds, is "not yet advanced enough."

Avdotya and Sitnikov get more raucous and shrill in their discussions of new theories, and at last Arkady can stand no more. "Gentlemen, it's getting something like Bedlam," he remarks. And with no leave-taking formalities the friends depart. Sitnikov hastens to follow them, eager to hear their opinion of Avdotya's "remarkable personality." Bazarov, of course, has nothing nice to say.

Comment

Turgenev takes no pains to hide his great contempt for Mme. Kukshin's variety of empty liberalism. Her room is the antithesis of femininity with its clutter of magazines, dust and cigarette butts. Her person is repugnantly disheveled; her ideas, haphazard and derivative. She is a caricature of a free woman.

Bazarov's reaction to Kukshin speaks well for his serious devotion to his ideas. He is unimpressed by her bandying about of the latest theories and articles, and refuses to be drawn into her empty theorizing. Bazarov, no matter what else he may be, is a serious and dedicated student of ideas and has no need to show off his erudition or parade his "freedom."

And yet, despicable as she may be as a woman of ideas, Avdotya is not a mean person. She is nervous and unkempt but yet generous and eager to please. Bazarov's rude, cruel treatment of her (deprecating her looks, yawning at her speeches) is unnecessary. He is, after all, freely drinking her champagne and enjoying her hospitality. He could have dismissed her prattling with a gentler hand. But we have learned by now that consideration is not one of Bazarov's strong points.

In all, this chapter, farcical in its setting and in its dialogue, is a great **parody** of the liberal salon. We can laugh out loud at Avdotya's and Sitnikov's pretensions and at the same time wonder where the middle road lies between the foolish official Matvy and the foolish emancipee Avdotya.

CHAPTER XIV

At the Governor's ball a few days later, Matvy Ilyitch is the model of graciousness, greeting all comers according to their importance. Arkady, who dances badly, and Bazarov who dances not at all, stand in the corner watching the dancers. Suddenly Sitnikov, who is standing with them, announces: "Odintsova is here!"

Arkady is immediately taken with the striking woman. She is graceful, dignified and tranquil. Sitnikov brings Arkady to Mme. Odintsov for an introduction and, although she is only a few years older than he, she makes him feel somehow like a schoolboy. While she dances with others, Arkady cannot take his eyes off her. Finally, they sit together on the side. At first Arkady is extremely shy, but Mme. Odintsov draws him out and he is soon prattling on about his family, school, studies and his friends Bazarov, whom Mme. Odintsov has remarked upon. While Arkady is breathlessly drawn to the lady, she treats him with gentle condescension.

They talk for almost an hour, and as Mme. Odintsoo rises to leave, she invites Arkady to come visit her. "Bring your friend with you," she adds. "I shall be very curious to see the man who has the courage to believe in nothing."

As soon as she leaves, Bazarov comes over, obviously impressed in his cynical way with Mme. Odintsov's appearance. "Whatever she may be ... she's got a pair of shoulders such as I've not set eyes on for a long while," he observes. Arkady is wounded by his cynicism, but unwilling to criticize, he changes the subject. The two agree to pay the lovely lady a visit.

Comment

Before he has Mme. Odintsov arrive at the ball, Turgenev manages to ridicule, through small detail, a provincial town all dressed up for a gala. The Governor "even while he remained perfectly motionless, was still 'making arrangements.'" Matvy "was all bows and smiles ... before the ladies," and let out hearty, unshared laughs "such as befits a high official." One officer, who had "spent six weeks in Paris," was doing all the appropriate dance steps with accompanying French shouts.

With Mme. Odintsov's entrance, all everyone's attention is centered on her. She is the essence of intelligent grace and charm. Everything about her is dignified and womanly. Bazarov is as much taken with her as Arkady. But his gruff pose insists that he make light of her virtue and appeal. He could never, as Arkady did, succumb publicly and unabashedly to his romantic stirrings.

CHAPTER XV

On the following day the two friends call on Mme. Odintsov at her hotel in town. Bazarov has heard, through town gossip, that Mme. Odintsov had been married to a rich old man and that her reputation for virtue is somewhat tarnished. He looks forward eagerly to the meeting.

As soon as Arkady introduces Bazarov to the lady, he notices with amazement that his friend seems embarrassed. To compensate for his embarrassment, Bazarov lolls in a chair and talks in exaggerated tones. Mme. Odintsov remains clam and tranquil.

Anna Sergyevna Odintsov is the daughter of a magnificent gambler who, after making a sensation in Moscow and St. Petersburg, ended in ruin in the countryside. When he died he left Anna who was 20 and a younger daughter Katya who was 12. Their mother had died years before. Anna had been educated brilliantly but she was not equipped to run a household in an isolated countryside. She sent for a dreadful aunt, Avdotya Stepanovna H-. and this arrogant, spiteful lady came to live with them.

Anna had begun to reconcile herself to a life in the wilds tending to her aunt and sister, when she met Odintsov, a very wealthy older man, "stout, heavy and sour." She married him, and on his death he willed her a fortune. She now lives in his house, Nikolskoe, thirty miles outside the town of X-.

The neighbors do not like the elegant Mme. Odintsov. They spread scandalous gossip about her virtue and resent her aloofness.

But as she meets in the hotel with the two young men she is easy and gracious. Bazarov is flustered. He talks a great deal, but not about his "ideas." As he talks of medicine, botany and science, Mme. Odintsov listens attentively, contributing intelligently to the conversation.

As for the smitten Arkady, she treats him like a sweet younger brother.

Three hours later the friends leave with an invitation to visit Anna at Nikolskoe. Bazarov, posing before his friend, says after they leave: "What a magnificent body ... Shouldn't I like to see it on the dissecting table!"

They decide to go to Nikolskoe and three days later they set off. It is June 22, Bazarov's Saint's Day (the Russian equivalent of our birthday). He muses to Arkady that "today they expect me home ... well, they can go on expecting ... what does it matter!"

Comment

Anna Odintsov is presented by Turgenev with complete sympathy. She at once perceives Bazarov's nervousness, and while his bad manners impress her unpleasantly she graciously makes exception for him and pays him her quiet attention. Anna's story is a sad and lonely one. Her marriage to the stout landowner was from necessity not greed and her ability to survive gracefully the hard vicissitudes of her life testify to her capabilities and inner tranquility.

Bazarov presents, once again, his two guises. His uneasiness and embarrassment before the gentle and intelligent woman is surprising and moving. He seems to be truly at a loss without his gruff guise. When Mme. Odintsov refuses to be offended by him, he becomes a charming and educated companion. As soon as they leave her hotel, however, he puts on his familiar "nihilism" for his "student" Arkady. Arkady reacts intensely to his cynicism, not only because he finds it crude and unmannerly, but because he has succumbed totally to Anna's charms. Arkady resents his treatment as a younger brother in Anna's presence, and notices with amazement Anna's attention to Bazarov and the nihilist's tell-tale embarrassment by her attention.

We could be all sympathy for Bazarov and his sweet unease-but Turgenev does not permit it. At the tag end of the chapter he introduces the thoughtless, callous side of his hero-his total disconcern for his parents' anxiety, his submission to his own desires at the cost of what can only be devastating disappointment for his waiting parents.

CHAPTER XVI

Anna Sergyevna's house is elegant, old-fashioned and well run. After the two friends are installed comfortably in their quarters, they go down to their hostess who introduces them to her "household." Katya, her younger sister, is charming, sweet and candid. "She was constantly blushing and getting out of breath."

The Princess, Anna's old aunt, is thin, pinched and ill-natured. She continually complains and while the sisters do everything possible to make her comfortable, they have learned how to politely ignore her prattle.

After tea, a neighbor, Porfiry Platonitch, "a stoutish, grayish man with short, spindly legs" comes visiting in search of a game of cards. Anna, the Princess and Bazarov play with him, while Arkady, oppressed at his "dismissal," is sent across the room to listen to Katya play the piano.

Katya is very shy with Arkady, and while he finds her pleasant enough, he longs to return to Anna's company. At night, when the friends have retired to their room, they share impressions. Arkady exclaims: "What an exquisite woman Anna Sergyevna is!" But Bazarov is cooler: "Yes ... a female with brains. Yes, and she's seen life too ... I'm convinced she manages her estate capitally too. But what's splendid is not her, but her sister."

Bazarov suggests that Arkady might "make something fine out of her." Arkady is unconvinced and uninterested.

Anna too mulls over the day. Finding Bazarov "something new," she is curious about him. But, as Turgenev describes Anna Sergyevna, she is "a rather strange creature." She is curious about many things, but she has neither sought nor found complete satisfaction. Her life, since her husband's death, has been comfortable if lonely and only occasionally do her physical and intellectual passions rise to the surface-to be brushed away quickly by the practical concerns of her well-ordered daily routine. Her experiences with the repugnant Odintsov have left her wary of all men. She sees them as "slovenly, heavy, drowsy and feebly importunate creatures." But yet she is somehow unfulfilled and dissatisfied. "This doctor is a strange man!" she thinks, as she falls off to sleep.

The next day, Anna goes off on a botany tour with Bazarov. Arkady, left alone, broods over his exclusion. He spends a little time with Katya but waits only to catch a glimpse of his hostess, who barely notices him when she returns from her walk.

Comment

We learn a great deal about Anna Sergyevna as we meet her at her estate. Her household is extremely well ordered, immaculate and comfortable. At 29, she has clearly mastered the complicated business of keeping a large estate in efficient order. Although the furnishings show the mark of her husband - luxurious "but without particularly good taste" - Anna's personal appearance is charming and tasteful. She handles the assorted members of her household with a firm but tactful hand. With Katya she is protective and at the same time imperious. Having raised and educated her younger sister, Anna Sergyevna feels free to order her about. That Katya is overawed by Anna is a possibility that has never entered Anna's mind. Anna treats her impossible aunt with total seeming respect and indulgence, yet never allows the cantankerous Princess to get in her way. It is a tribute to Anna's detachment, to her refusal to involve herself totally, that she has learned to manage her difficult and tedious daily life.

With Bazarov, Anna is provocative, attentive and unyielding. She counters his arguments skillfully, and matches his directness with her own. She disagrees with his proposal that all men are alike, that "a single human specimen is sufficient to judge all by," but she disagrees graciously, intelligently and with the assertiveness of a true emancipee.

Anna is affected by Bazarov. But she is a detached, highly controlled and selfish woman whose great disappointments and passions are hidden far below the surfaces of calm, order and propriety. We begin to suspect that Bazarov has more than met his match.

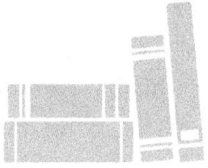

FATHERS AND SONS

TEXTUAL ANALYSIS

CHAPTERS 17 - 23

CHAPTER XVII

Time passes very rapidly for the two friends as they fall into the precisely ordered routine of Anna's estate. Almost without their being aware of it, two weeks fly by. Arkady has determined conclusively that he is in love with Mme. Odintsov, but since she shunts him off he finds solace in the constant companionship of Katya. Bazarov, for his part, is at home with his hostess and usually the days are spent with the two couples going their separate ways.

Bazarov, in two weeks, has undergone subtle change. He is irritable and sometimes taciturn. He is "tortured and maddened" by his feelings for Anna. He has always been of the opinion that "If a woman takes your fancy, try and gain your end; but if you can't-well, turn your back on her - there are lots of good fish in the sea." Although Anna has taken his fancy and unmistakably likes him, he sees that it is impossible to "gain his ends" and equally impossible to turn his back on her. He is tortured by his desire for her and is furious at his own idealism concerning her.

Anna enjoys being with Bazarov, and when he suddenly announces one day that he is leaving for his father's house, "she turned white, as though something had given her a pang." That same evening Anna and Bazarov find themselves alone in Anna's room. She asks him why he is leaving. "And why stay?" is his retort. An excruciating tense and flirtatious scene follows. Bazarov is racked by his desire for Anna, and she leads him on, toying with the possibilities. This is a "new" Bazarov, a young man in the torments of desire. "I'm surprised that so far you ... have not found what you wanted," he tells her in response to her statement that her idea of love is "everything or nothing. A life for a life. Take mine, give up thine." "And do you think it would be easy to give oneself up wholly to anything whatever?" she asks. Not if you "begin reflecting, waiting and attaching value to yourself," he reasons.

The tensions become unbearable and as Bazarov moves to go, Mme. Odintsov whispers, "Wait a little." Bazarov suddenly goes up to her, says "good-bye" and squeezes her hand "so that she almost screamed."

Long after he leaves, Anna sits without moving in her chair. Bazarov goes for a long, ill-tempered walk and is annoyed, on his return, to find Arkady still awake in their room.

Comment

In this tense and unresolved interview we have convincing proof that Turgenev, as he himself insisted, is dealing primarily with people and not ideas. We are greatly moved by Bazarov's struggle with himself, by his wrestling with unfamiliar phenomena. He becomes, through his anguish, a very real character and not merely a prototype of the "new man."

He wants Anna physically, and, we suspect, spiritually, with a devastating intensity. He writhes at the realization that she is "playing" with him, although she herself is stirred by his passion. Bazarov struggles throughout this interview, as he has during his two-week visit, to remain detached and cynical. Alone, he berates himself for succumbing to his "romanticism," but in public (before Anna) he displays a "calm contempt for everything idealistic."

What we are seeing is a love relationship far removed from the ordinary courtship patterns. Katya and Arkady's relationship is proceeding quietly and in the expected manner. But Anna is wrestling with her long practiced reserve and Bazarov with his consuming ideologies. The difficulties they encounter in making contact are absorbing and unexpected.

CHAPTER XVIII

The following morning, Anna and Bazarov carefully avoid each other. Then suddenly Anna appears in the drawing room and asks Bazarov to come to her room to discuss a textbook he had mentioned to her the day before. They sit in the same chairs as they had the night before and Mme. Odintsov suddenly stretches out her hand: "I wanted to continue our conversation of last night. You went away so suddenly ..." she brings out. "But what were we talking about last night?" he counters coyly. "We were talking of happiness, I believe," she replies.

Anna asks him what he really wants from his life. But Bazarov cannot open up to her. "Between you and me there is such a gulf," he protests. Anna presses harder, and the conversation soon reactivates the tension of the night before. She pushes him to tell her what is on his mind right now, exhorts him to shed his reticence. He finally relents in a rush of words: "Let me tell you then that I love you like a fool, like a madman... There, you've forced it out of me."

Anna makes no reply but to utter his name with a "ring of unconscious tenderness in her voice." Bazarov, able to bear no more, rushes to her and draws her to him. In an instant she is across the room. "You have misunderstood me," she whispers hurriedly. Bazarov, biting his lips, leaves quickly.

Later in the day he sends a note asking if he can stay till tomorrow. "Why should you go? I did not understand you-you did not understand me," is her reply.

Alone with her thoughts all afternoon, Anna drifts between blaming herself for pushing Bazarov, toying with the idea of relenting, and finally deciding: "God knows what it would lead to; he [can't] be played with; peace is anyway the best thing in the world."

Although her peace of mind is not ultimately shaken, Anna feels gloomy all day. She has "forced herself to look behind herself, and had seen behind her not even an abyss, but what was empty ... or revolting."

Comment

This resolution of the preceding night's interview is a sad one. Turgenev has maneuvered us into a position of great sympathy for Bazarov and we are hurt by his painful rejection.

The scene in Anna's bedroom, with Bazarov blurting his declaration as he faces the window, is so alive and so painful, it is hard not to speculate whether Turgenev himself had not once lived through such a scene. (See Introduction).

It is easy to understand why Anna goads Bazarov into his declaration. She is bored and lonely. She has kept her passions submerged for so long that she suddenly feels a great need to release them. Life, Anna feels, is passing her by. She has had no change in the rigid routine for so long. Bazarov is attractive and he excites her. But the force of his passion, the depth of his intensity, frightens her, and she involuntarily recoils-it is not a commitment she is willing to take on. It does not take Anna long to regain her composure and peace of mind-a tribute to the efficacy of her repression. She perhaps would have liked to respond to Bazarov, but the vision she has of the disruption of her hard-earned peace and ease horrifies and repulses her.

CHAPTER XIX

Dinner that night is awkward and strained. Bazarov is gloomy and contemptuous of the whole company. After dinner Anna and Bazarov find themselves alone in the garden. Bazarov apologizes to Anna, who insists she is not angry but "sorry."

Bazarov announces he is leaving the next day. "You don't love me, and you never will love me, I suppose," he muses. And that would be the only condition under which he could stay. Anna suddenly thinks: "I'm afraid of this man," and sensing her fear, Bazarov abruptly says good-bye. As the tension mounts through the day, much to Arkady's confusion (he has no idea of what has happened) the household is suddenly relieved by the unexpected arrival of the "modern man," Sitnikov. Introducing, as he does, the element of commonplace reality, he affords relief to the isolated and embroiled "couples."

When they retire that night, Bazarov informs Arkady of his intension of leaving the next day. Relations are by now so strained between the friends that they cannot discuss the cause of the sudden departure. Arkady decides to leave also. Although he dreads leaving Anna's house, losing the chance to be near her, he is also sorry to have to leave Katya. So sorry, that in the quiet of the night he sheds a few tears.

The next morning Arkady is convinced that he should go in Sitnikov's carriage, while Bazarov will borrow Arkady's coach and head for his home. After they have gone a little way, Arkady feels a great desire to be with his friend, and at a stop he suddenly transfers to Bazarov's coach and asks to be taken along.

The two young men, temporarily at peace, maintain an absorbed silence throughout the trip. Bazarov once interrupts the silence to speak of how foolish they both have been to be mastered by a woman: "To my mind, it's better to break stones on the high road than to let a woman have the mastery of even the end of one's little finger." "A man ought not to be tame," he concludes.

As they draw near Bazarov's home, after a trip that seems interminable to Arkady, they see Bazarov's father in the distance, eagerly awaiting the coach's arrival.

Comment

A great change has-taken place in the relationship between Arkady and Bazarov. Before they visited Anna, they were friends on near equal footing. Bazarov, the elder of the two, was always the intellectual tutor but they shared unhesitatingly their thoughts and feelings. With Bazarov's tormented involvement with Anna, and Arkady's schoolboy crush on her, it became impossible for the young men to speak freely. Arkady is melancholy and self-pitying; Bazarov, ashamed and furious.

The night before they leave Anna's, Arkady attempts to banter with Bazarov - "which is always an unmistakable sign of secret displeasure or unexpressed suspicions."

As Arkady tries to make conversation with Bazarov, bringing up the foolish Sitnikov for ridicule, Bazarov snaps: "You're still a fool, my boy, I see. Sitnikovs are indispensable to us ... I need dolts like him. It's not for the gods to bake bricks..." Suddenly "all the fathomless depths of Bazarov's conceit" dawns on Arkady. "You're a god; am not I a dolt then?" asks Arkady sarcastically. "Yes," comes the answer, "you're still a fool."

Under stress, the great attachment of the young friends does not hold up. They are in different leagues. Bazarov is, in fact, too tempestuous, iconoclastic and cynical for Arkady. And as Arkady begins to feel an independent strength of his own, he begins also to find fault with Bazarov.

Yet, Arkady's impetuous move to join Bazarov midway on the trip is evidence of his great attachment to his "mentor." Arkady wants to be with Bazarov, is still drawn and fascinated by the nihilist's powerful and compelling philosophy. When Bazarov launches into his tirade against man's being mastered by woman, he includes Arkady in his own category of foolishness. The young men have made their temporary peace. But the master has revealed cracks in his perfect armor, and the pupil, signs of discontent.

CHAPTER XX

The introduction to Bazarov's family is a **parody**, not altogether unloving, of the outdated generation of provincial fathers. Bazarov's mother, Arina Vlasyevna, is unabashedly old-fashioned. She throws herself at her son with great sobs of joy when he dismounts from the carriage. She fusses, gazes in rapture, embraces, gushes emotion. Her great concern is to feed Bazarov well and make him comfortable so that he will not leave for a while. At the end of the chapter Turgenev includes a lighthearted description of Arina as "a genuine Russian gentlewoman of the olden times." She is highly superstitious, extremely devout without questioning. She never reads a book but is great at housewifery. She shudders at "modern" theories, but is generous with her servants. But above all she loves her son and fears him "unutterably." Highly volatile and emotional, Arina Vlasyevna is constantly "expecting some great misfortune," concludes Turgenev. "Such women are not common nowadays. God knows whether we ought to rejoice!"

Vassily Ivanovitch, Bazarov's father, is more complicated than his wife and desperately eager to please his son on the young man's terms. He attempts to appear indifferent to Bazarov's return, but his twitching eyebrows and quivering beard give him away. When he speaks to the young men he is at once touchingly apologetic and proud of his mistaken "modernity." To please his son and Arkady, Vassily Ivanovitch bills himself as a "thinking man" who has tried "not to get rusty ... not to fall behind the age." The old man is pathetic in his attempts to impress his son. In striving to appear au courant Vassily quotes sources that Bazarov has long since discarded, and when he attempts a humorous anecdote it comes out as village gossip.

Vassily continually apologizes for his humble "estate," for the lack of space in the house. He is desperate to make the young men comfortable, to please them, and to win their approval. Bazarov will offer him no solace. He criticizes his father's mannerisms, makes no attempt to conceal his contempt for the old man's out-of-date ideas, and in general behaves as rudely and off-handedly with his doting parents as if they were inconsequential strangers.

Comment

With the young men's arrival at Bazarov's home Turgenev begins the fourth major section of the book. His gently mocking portrayal of the old Bazarovs at once disparages their foolishness and arouses great sympathy for their tenderness and humility.

Old Bazarov, so easily mocked and dismissed by his son, is gentle, loving and slightly ridiculous. His greatest desire is to please his son and be worthy of his esteem. Bazarov's rudeness to him once again hardens us against the young nihilist. During his anguish over Anna we had forgotten how cruel and abrupt he could be. This chapter, perhaps more than any other in the book, displays the timelessness of Turgenev's **theme**. Bazarov is the prototype of the young man returning home after an absence with a fully formed philosophy of his own who finds his parents old-fashioned and vaguely ridiculous. Little habits and pretensions, overlooked in youth, suddenly become intolerable. The young man is forced into a disquieting recognition of his parents' inadequacies. He is ashamed of their provincialism, their failure to keep apace of "progress." It is the typical reaction of a young person against the older generation. Turgenev's great talent lies in describing the process with such sympathetic insight and detail.

There are a host of little matters in the chapter which gathered together form an insurmountable barrier between the generations. If we look at a few of them we will see how brilliantly and delicately Turgenev managed this complicated relationship:

- As soon as old Bazarov meets Arkady he apologizes for the simplicity of his household: "everything in my house is done in a plain way." Arkady's father had made much the same apology to Bazarov–neither parent realizes that the young men are not concerned with elaborate surroundings.

- When old Bazarov asks Tanyusha, a young serving girl, to bring his wife a glass of water he adds: "on a tray, do you hear?" Clearly trays are not ordinarily used in the Bazarov house and it is a gesture meant to impress (though it does just the contrary) the young men.

- Vassily flourishes a "new yellow silk handkerchief" which he has snatched up behind the boys' backs. He means to show his "style" but we can imagine young Bazarov's expression upon seeing this unaccustomed finery.

- On ordinary days old Bazarov had in attendance at dinner a serf boy who drove away the flies with a branch. "But on this occasion ... [he] had sent him away through dread of the criticism of the younger generation." Of course, the flies were the main irritant for the young men during the meal.

- When Bazarov's mother kisses him good night she embraces him "and stealthily behind his back she [gives] him her blessing three times." Had Bazarov seen that blessing, his reaction would have doubtless been profane and wounding.

In all, this chapter is one of the most moving in the book. It is so viable, so contemporary, so sympathetic that we cannot doubt for a moment that, while Turgenev's head was with the younger generation, his heart was surely with the older.

CHAPTER XXI

The morning after their arrival, Arkady has a long chat with old Bazarov. He assures the delighted old man that his son will someday be famous and that Bazarov "is one of the most remarkable men I have ever met," As they join in praises of young Bazarov, the old man says he has only one ambition - that there be a line in Bazarov's biography saying: "The son of a simple army doctor, who was, however, capable of divining his greatness betimes, and spared nothing for his education."

Later in the day, Bazarov and Arkady rest on a pile of hay in the shade. They speak of Bazarov's childhood, of the simplicity and rewards of his parents' lives, of Bazarov's despair at occupying so tiny a space "in comparison with the rest of space," and of his anger at being rejected by Anna Sergyevna. As the conversation goes on, Bazarov begins to goad and needle Arkady: "You are a soft-hearted mawkish creature... You're timid; you don't rely on yourself much." "Have you a high opinion of yourself," asks Arkady. "When I meet a man who can hold his own beside me ... then I'll change my opinion of myself," answers Bazarov.

In deliberate provocation of Arkady, Bazarov begins to disparage Arkady's uncle Pavel. Arkady responds with fury and the two young friends, both violently angry, are about to fight. They are interrupted at the peak of animosity by Vassily who has come to call them to dinner. Vassily innocently joins them for a moment, and as he chats about the old days in the Army, young Bazarov falls asleep in his face.

The village priest has been invited by Arina to dinner and after the meal he soundly downs Bazarov at a game of whist.

The following day, Bazarov announces to Arkady that he will leave the next morning. He cannot work here, while "in your house one can at any rate shut oneself up." But even Bazarov has difficulty in breaking the news of his sudden departure to his parents. He delays the announcement all day and finally at night he says, "with a feigned yawn" to his father: "Oh ... I was almost forgetting to tell you... Send .. for our horses tomorrow." The old man is dumbfounded and heartbroken. He naturally makes but a feeble protest: "Three days ... after three years, it's rather little." Old Bazarov spares his wife the news until morning. She, like her husband, is "utterly crushed."

When Bazarov tears himself away the next morning, the two old people feel the burden of their great solitude. 'He has cast us off ... forsaken us, he was dull with us," falters the old man. And his wife, with a new-found stoicism, comforts him: "A son is a separate pieces cut off. He's like the falcon that flies home and flies away at his pleasure... Only I am left you unchanged forever, as you for me."

Comment

The two major scenes in this long chapter are both highly charged with emotion, and are extremely moving in different ways. The quarrel between the friends on the haystack shows us the depth of their involvement with their ideas and, on Bazarov's part, the pain of his wound from Anna's rejection.

Bazarov, ashamed of his submission to romantic love, is beginning to doubt his own importance in the universe. His dedication to great principles has, after all, made him no greater than any other man. The existence of this doubt frightens him, and the fear, coupled with his painful memory of Anna, makes him irritable and provoking. He does not hate Arkady, although he hates something that day with enough force to bring him to the edge of violence. Bazarov's great assurance is frayed at the edges - and the recognition of the fraying is painful and leaves him frantic with a sense of his own impotence. Turgenev is sympathetic with Bazarov's fury and frustration - the depth of which shows in Bazarov's face as he prepares to attack Arkady.

But Turgenev is not sympathetic with the pain Bazarov inflicts on his parents. The reaction of the old people to their son's abrupt departure is so moving, so pathetically brave, that we loathe Bazarov for bringing on their desolation. The final scene, with the old people returning to their shrinking house, made small by Bazarov's departure, is magnificent in its simplicity and evocation of utter anguish.

As pathetic as that final tableau is, Turgenev, ultimately, poses a problem rather than passes judgment. It really is inevitable, he tells us through Arina; the young must really fly away. What little solace it may bring our old Bazarovs at the moment it is the way of the world - the way of fathers and sons.

Anyone who accuses Turgenev of writing a political tract or a philosophical dialogue in *Fathers and Sons* need only turn to this chapter to see how committed the author was to the emotions of his characters, to the life of the individual. Turgenev was a creative writer first, a recorded of history and ideas second.

CHAPTER XXII

In silence, the young friends travel toward Maryino. At one point they decide on impulse to stop in at Mme. Odintsov's. The impulse proves folly and within four hours they are on their way again, having exchanged only awkward conversation with Anna.

Their reception the next day at Maryino is, by contrast, warm and excited. Even Pavel seems glad to have the wanderers back. Conditions on the farm, however, have worsened. Both hired hands and peasants are thieving, drinking and quarreling, and Nikolai Petrovitch is at a loss as to how to control matters.

Bazarov sets to work at Maryino, but Arkady is restless and bored. After ten days he suddenly gallops off to town and from there to Anna's estate. When he arrives at Nikolskoe he comes upon Katya in the garden. She flushes with delight at his return and brings him directly to her sister. Anna welcomes him warmly and with apparent pleasure.

Comment

The three events of this transitional chapter tie together the three major sections which have preceded it. The abortive visit to Nikolskoe reintroduces Anna and Katya into the mainstream of the story. The stay at Maryino, with its ever increasing difficulties, returns us to Nikolai's farm problems and the inadequacies of the older generation. And Arkady's flight to Nikolskoe looks forward to the fulfillment of the love story.

Technically this chapter unites the disparate segments of the book. We have been given all the necessary **exposition**; we have seen life at the three households. From this point on, Turgenev will attempt to deal with the problems posed in the expository chapters.

CHAPTER XXIII

In Arkady's absence, Bazarov continues his research at Maryino. Pavel, whose loathing for the man has grown, if possible, greater, carefully avoids any arguments with the young nihilist. Nikolai Petrovitch comes regularly to observe Bazarov's experiments. And Fenitchka and Bazarov, over the days, become fast and easy friends.

One day, when Fenitchka is in the arbor, Bazarov comes upon her and begins flirting with the charming young innocent. She responds guilelessly to the flirtation and when Bazarov finally bends down to kiss her she pushes him away-feebly. Just then, Pavel, of whom Fenitchka is more than ever afraid, enters the arbor. The couple separate quickly as Pavel hisses maliciously: "You are here."

Bazarov later remembers with "shame and contemptuous annoyance" another similar scene. But he soon shakes off his annoyance. Pavel for his part goes with great deliberation to the woods, where he stays, gloomily brooding, for a long while.

Comment

The flirtatious garden scene between Fenitchka and Bazarov is so charming, and on her part so innocent, that its naturalness rather than its deceitfulness is what remains with us.

We are prepared for Pavel's appearance by an earlier description of his behavior concerning Fenitchka. "For some time he had begun to watch her, and would suddenly make his appearance, as though he sprang out of the earth behind her back, in his English suit, with his immovable vigilant face, and his hands in his pockets."

Bazarov is responding to the lovely Fenitchka quite naturally and with no pretension. He makes her so comfortable through his own ease that she is more at home with him than with Nikolai Petrovitch himself.

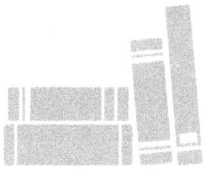

FATHERS AND SONS

TEXTUAL ANALYSIS

CHAPTERS 23 - 28

CHAPTER XXIV

Two hours after he has returned from his gloomy walk in the woods, Pavel appears at Bazarov's study door. In sarcastically formal language, the elegant gentleman challenges the young nihilist to a duel. Bazarov, with great irony and derision, accepts the challenge. Accordingly, the next morning they meet in a secluded corner of the woods, and with the petrified servant Piotr as witness they pace off the agreed upon distance and take aim with their pistols. Pavel fires a shot which misses, and then Bazarov, quite by chance and without taking aim, fires and hits Pavel in the thigh. Bazarov throws down his pistol and assuming the role of doctor tends to Pavel's wound, which does not appear to be dangerous.

Within an hour Pavel is lying in his bed with his leg skillfully bandaged. During the night his fever rises and the next morning, in somewhat of a delirium, he whispers to his brother: "Don't you think, Nikolai, Fenitchka has something in common with Nellie?" "What Nellie, Pavel dear," asks his brother. "How can you ask? Princess R - ... C'est de la meme famille." Nikolai marvels at the persistence of old feeling, and suspects nothing even when Pavel moans: "Ah, how I loved that light-headed creature! ... I can't bear any insolent upstart to dare to touch ..."

As Bazarov prepares to leave, having first released all his insects and frogs, Pavel calls for him and the two men icily shake hands.

Pavel has to stay in bed for a week and Fenitchka, with great dread, waits on him. Every time she enters the room Pavel stares at her with strange intensity. One day as she is about to leave his room, Pavel begins to question her about her feelings for Nikolai. Do you love him "with your whole soul, with your whole heart?" He presses her urgently: "And you will never give him up for anyone?" He brings up that day in the arbor, but Fenitchka swears her innocence.

In a great spasm of emotion Pavel whispers, "love him, love my brother! ... Think what can be more terrible than to love and not be loved! ..." Suddenly Pavel takes her hand and with great sighs clings to it. "At that instant his whole ruined life stirred up within him."

The searing moment finally ends with Nikolai's approach. Fenitchka leaves hurriedly in secret terror, and Pavel with great vehemence exhorts his brother to marry her: "Put an end to the scandal and bad example you are setting." Nikolai, who has always feared his brother's aristocratic reproaches at such a liaison, agrees with much excitement. The brothers embrace with feeling. When Nikolai leaves, Pavel lies back on his perfumed pillow and in the glaring daylight his head "lay on the white pillow like the head of a dead man ... and indeed he was a dead man."

Comment

This rapidly shifting chapter is complex and yet compact. We are given a vast amount of plot, emotion and characterization. The scene in which Pavel makes the challenge brings to a peak the conflict of the generations. It is not only Bazarov whom Pavel despises, but the whole way of life he represents. The duel itself is ironically comical, almost farcical. Neither party really wants it, and yet both must fight for their life in this poetic, anachronistic fashion.

Pavel, on his sick bed, is wracked by the passions of his devastated life. Fenitchka, as the embodiment of his "lost" Princess, evokes all his self-pity and provokes all his suppressed passion. His advice to Nikolai at once reconciles him to his own misfortunes and to the liberal mood of the new generation.

Turgenev's description of Pavel as a "dead man" is a metaphoric one. He does not actually die. But with the relinquishing of his passion for Fenitchka he relinquishes his life's passions and nothing remains but the appearance of a living being.

Dueling, in the 1860s, was still a fairly common method of settling passionate grievances. But it was a practice among the chivalrous and urbane attended by strict rules and procedures. The elaborate chivalric intricacies of the duel - the formal challenge, the appointment, the choice of weapons, the seconds - are comically out of place on a provincial farm. Of all the characters, Pavel is the only one who would dream of a duel. His affected, aristocratic mannerisms are shown in all their foolishness when he fights the losing duel at this time and this place.

As ludicrous as the duel is at Maryino, it is important to remember that dueling was a serious, passionate matter in 1860. Only a generation before, two of Russia's greatest writers, Pushkin and Lermentov, had been killed in duels. And Turgenev himself was challenged to a duel by Tolstoy (fortunately the duel was never fought). As late as 1901, Chekhov was able to write a realistic play (*The Three Sisters*) in which one of the characters was killed in a duel.

The duel was a dramatic and dangerous expression of passion, and Pavel's challenge to Bazarov is so out of place, so ludicrously extreme and concludes so absurdly that we are forced to laugh at his "manners" rather than sympathize with his torment.

CHAPTER XXV

At Nikolskoe, unaware of the events at Maryino, Arkady and Katya's romance blossoms. They sit together in the garden, in a silence "expressive of confidential intimacy."

Arkady has changed since his arrival at Nikolskoe. His "satirical tendencies" have disappeared and he is at peace. He confesses to Katya that he has always been a little afraid of Anna, and she tells him that he is not like Bazarov-he is "tame" while Bazarov is "wild" and "full of force."

As their talk grows personal, Arkady tells Katya that he puts her "not only above your sister, but above everyone in the world." Embarrassed by his declaration he abruptly leaves her and Katya is left alone in the garden, a "crimson flush" on her face.

Returning to the house, Arkady learns that Bazarov awaits him in his room. Bazarov tells Arkady of the duel and then begins to needle him about his "affair" with Anna Sergyevna. Arkady is indignant at the accusation and hurt when Bazarov declares that it is evident their friendship is over.

When Anna learns of Bazarov's presence, she summons him and in a tense, cryptic interview they both agree that all is forgiven and forgotten. "They both supposed they were speaking truth," observes Turgenev. "Was ... the whole truth to be found in their words? They could not themselves have said, and much less could the author."

Anna tells Bazarov how "clever" and enjoyable she now finds Arkady, and in irritation, Bazarov blurts: "It is probably no secret to you that he was in love with you?" Involuntarily she exclaims: "What! he too?" While Anna and Bazarov have their charged conversation, Arkady sits in the garden "wondering and rejoicing, and resolving on something."

Comment

The general peacefulness of this chapter comes as a relief after the tumult of the one preceding it. Arkady and Katya's growing romance is charming and gentle. His realization that he feels no jealousy of Anna and Bazarov resolves that misplaced passion. The uneasy peace between Anna and Bazarov resolves, at least on the surface, their ill-starred romance. And the termination of the uneven intimacy between the two young men dissolves a friendship which was not altogether constructive or productive.

CHAPTER XXVI

The day after Bazarov's arrival Arkady tries, in a secluded stone house in the garden, to tell Katya of his love for her. But he stammers and hedges and cannot say what he wants. Suddenly Bazarov and Anna walk by and unaware that the "young people" are just behind the hedge, they continue a conversation they have been having.

They talk of themselves and then of Arkady. Anna says: "I have come to think more often of him. In such youthful, fresh feeling there is a special charm..." Bazarov, jealous and spiteful, goads her about Arkady. When they pass out of earshot, Arkady turns with passion to Katya and declares his love and proposes. With charming grace she accepts.

Arkady sends a note to Anna Sergyevna asking for Katya's hand. Anna summons Bazarov and they discuss the proposal. They agree that it will be a satisfactory marriage, and somewhat ironically conclude that they are already out of touch with the generation behind them.

Bazarov says good-bye to Anna and she suddenly feels pity for the man who loved her, but he will tolerate no sympathy. In saying good-bye to Arkady, Bazarov is harsh and irrevocable. "It's useless to deceive ourselves-we are parting for good..." he declares. "You're not made for our bitter, rough, lonely existence. There's no dash, no hate in you ... you gentry can never get beyond refined submission or refined indignation." Bazarov goes on berating Arkady for his "softness." Although the ex-disciple is upset at the moment, as soon as Bazarov leaves, Arkady finds consolation in Katya and a few hours later he has forgotten his former teacher.

Anna, too, after a little while, "set her own mind at rest," realizing that her feelings for Arkady had been "curiosity, nothing but curiosity, and love of ease, and egoism."

Comment

There is somehow a shadow of doom cast over Bazarov in this chapter of happiness for Arkady. The woman he loves (or loved) admits her attraction to Arkady; his young disciple is finding happiness down another road from his, and he is setting off alone, harsh and disappointed.

A shadow also falls over Anna. Although only 29, she is already too old to have read the signs of love between the young people. Her guileless younger sister has won out in a demi-struggle, a struggle in which Anna's selfish passions ultimately failed to fascinate. To protect herself she withdraws once more into her tight, controlled, self-centered and passionless "peace."

CHAPTER XXVII

Bazarov returns to his overjoyed parents and immerses himself in his studies. But after a while he is beset by boredom and restlessness. "A strange weariness began to show itself in all his movements." His parents are terrified by his new kind of irritability. And when he seeks conversation with local peasants they leave him muttering: "O, he clacked away about something or other; wanted to stretch his tongue a bit. Of course, he's a gentleman; what does he understand?"

Finally, Bazarov begins to help his father in his medical practice and regains something of his old vigor. Then one day, Bazarov performs an autopsy on a peasant who has died of typhus. Bazarov suffers a small cut on his finger which he neglects, and within three days he begins to feel terribly ill. By the fourth day he is unable to get out of bed and the fever mounts. Bazarov finally admits to his father that he is dying of typhus. He begs the old man to send a message to Anna Sergyevna: "Yevgeny Bazarov ... sends his greetings and sends word he is dying." Old Bazarov sends the message. Meanwhile the young man approaches delirium, fighting desperately and bravely to keep his strength and wits.

Anna arrives the next day, bringing a doctor with her. When she sees Bazarov's inflamed and deathly face, "she felt simply dismayed, with a sort of cold and suffocating dismay." "This is royally done," Bazarov says to her when they are alone. "Monarchs, they say, visit the dying too." Bazarov tells her again how much he has loved her and when she sits beside him he protests: "I thought ... I wouldn't die ... there were problems to solve and I was a giant! And now all the problem for the giant is how to die decently."

In a final great passion, Bazarov begs Anna to "breath on the dying lamp, and let it go out." She kisses him on the forehead. "Enough," he murmurs, "now ... darkness." The following day Bazarov is dead.

Comment

Bazarov's death, pointlessly and carelessly caused, is enormously moving. The young man who was prepared to solve Russia's problems, ready to sacrifice for his ideals, is cut down for no reason. He dies bravely and nobly. Literary critics of the book have found fault with Bazarov's unexpected death. They accuse

Turgenev of failing to know what to do with the young nihilist. Political critics in Turgenev's time condemned the author for emasculating the young revolutionary, for making him seem foolish and worthless by killing him off so easily and pointlessly before he had accomplished anything.

But Bazarov is far from foolish at death. He dies magnificently. His nobility at death and his readiness to accept it are tributes to his strong will. He has changed nothing, he who wanted to change so much-so why not die. The power of the death scene apparently gripped Turgenev as strongly as it does his readers- he wept as he wrote it.

Above all, Bazarov's pointless death seems a positive and powerful symbol, not at all a negation of his philosophy. It is a symbol of a Russia as yet unprepared for him, the fault lying with Russia not the young revolutionary. It is a symbol of a Russia too backward in medicine to prevent his death, a backwardness which the young medical student decried and despised. It is a symbol for the young generation of reformers of what they must work for-a Russia advanced enough to accept, not crush, her mightiest men.

CHAPTER XXVIII

In this last chapter, Turgenev ties up loose ends. Within six months of Bazarov's death, Arkady marries Katya and Nikolai Petrovitch marries Fenitchka. All are stronger and happier. At a farewell dinner for Pavel (who is leaving for Moscow), each in their own way shows a new confidence.

Then, to satisfy the reader's curiosity, Turgenev follows his characters to the "actual present." Anna Sergyevna is married out of "good sense" not love to "one of the future leaders of Russia ... still young, good-natured and cold as ice." Anna's aunt, the Princess K-is dead: "forgotten the day of her death." Both pairs of Kirsanovs live at Maryino and under Arkady's careful management the farm is beginning to flourish. Katya has a son, "little Nikolai." Pavel, now in Dresden, is yet a perfect gentleman and is much sought after by tourists, but "life is a burden to him," and he is bitter.

Matvy Ilyitch, the petty official, is temporarily "in opposition." Mme. Kukshin, the false liberal, is in Heidelberg studying architecture and fraternizing with students. Sitnikov "roams about St. Petersburg" still "getting ready to be great." And Bazarov's feeble old parents, in great woe, visit his overgrown grave and the flowers blooming there speak of "eternal reconciliation and of life without end."

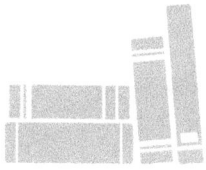

FATHERS AND SONS

A SPORTSMAN'S SKETCHES

From 1847 to 1851, Turgenev wrote 21 tales for a liberal magazine, *The Contemporary*. In 1852, these tales were collected and published as *A Sportsman's Sketches*. The book gained immediate popularity and has been compared in social impact to *Uncle Tom's Cabin*. (Alexander II reportedly attributed his partiality to emancipation to the impression the *Sketches* made on him.)

There is no unity of plot in the 21 sketches. They are loosely joined by a common narrator who meets the various characters while out on hunting expeditions. The object of the book is to give a realistic portrait of the peasants, to show them as human beings endowed with dignity, love, courage and ambition. Probably due to censorship, Turgenev avoided scenes of cruelty, abuse and violence. He concentrated, rather, on portrayal of character. While the peasants are given dignity amidst their cruel oppression, the landowners are gently and ironically mocked-never assaulted head-on.

With the publication of the *Sketches*, Turgenev became an important and acclaimed member of the Russian literati.

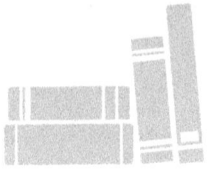

FATHERS AND SONS

RUDIN

Rudin was Turgenev's first full-length novel. Its hero, Rudin, is one of Turgenev's frequently characterized "superfluous men." The son of a petty squire, Rudin studies abroad and then returns to Russia a pure product of romantic idealism. He propagandizes and speechifies on freedom, beauty and sacrifice, but he is utterly incapable of taking action. He understands neither people nor ideas and he mistakes his dreams for accomplishments. As he fails to act politically so he also fails in love. Finally, homeless and useless, he goes to Paris where he is killed at the barricades in 1848.

Rudin is allegedly modeled on Mikhail Bakunin, the cerebral anarchist with the "cold heart."

FATHERS AND SONS

A NEST OF GENTLEFOLK

This book is in some senses a nostalgic ode to the disappearing world of aristocratic estates. Its hero, Fedor Lavretsky, reared in the Anglophile tradition of the aristocracy, is ill equipped to deal with the harsh realities of a changing Russia. Lavretsky marries a shallow and unfaithful girl whose desertion in Paris shocks and bewilders him. He returns to Russia and finds true love with a neighbor's daughter. They are devoted to each other but, just as they are to be married, the first wife, presumed dead, reappears. Lavretsky's true love is horrified at her own "adultery" and enters a nunnery. The wife departs again and Lavretsky is left alone, to an empty and lonely life.

Lavretsky is doomed to melancholy and unproductivity because of his unbreakable attachment to an aristocratic life that is no longer meaningful.

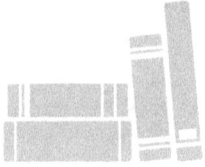

FATHERS AND SONS

ON THE EVE

The immediate predecessor of *Fathers and Sons*, this book portrays characters more tough-minded than their literary ancestors. The book marks the end of Turgenev's preoccupation with superfluous men who dwell in the past, and turns more to energetic characters eager for action.

Yelena, a strong-willed woman devoted to freedom and activity, rejects the suitors around her in favor of Insarov, a Bulgarian who has devoted himself to the liberation of Bulgaria from the Turkish oppressors. Insarov devotes himself passionately to his work and Yelena deserts family and fortune to marry him. After Insarov's premature death, Yelena remains in Europe, convinced that Russia is not yet capable of producing its own Insarovs.

Contemporary reviewers thought they saw in *On the Eve* the message that Russia someday soon would produce its own men of action. Turgenev objected to this interpretation-he resented the dicta of the new generation that even fiction should have its political messages and he bridled at their anti-esthetic tendencies.

FATHERS AND SONS

CHARACTER ANALYSES

Bazarov

Yevgeny Bazarov, a medical student in his late 20s, is a self-proclaimed "nihilist" (from the Latin nihil, nothing). He fervently believes that all existing institutions must be swept away, all traditions utterly destroyed, before a new life can be constructed in Russia. He deplores the aristocratic, the pseudo-intellectual and the sentimental. Bazarov is the central character, the focus of the book. All other characters are seen in relation to him, all traditions and philosophies measured in terms of his nihilism.

Bazarov is dynamic, almost animal-like in his strength and magnetism. He is fanatically devoted to his principles with a conviction that supplants human sympathy and understanding. At times, Bazarov seems almost inhuman. He is ruthless with his own family and Arkady's. He is insolent, rude, provocative and rough-mannered. He will tolerate no human foible. But he is fallible and not at all mechanical, and therefore he is ultimately very human. He falls madly and hopelessly in love; he has a flashing (if sarcastic) wit; he despairs of his failures, and he faces death with magnificent nobility.

As much as Bazarov's brusqueness may repel us, we are drawn to him-to his great convictions and readiness to sacrifice, to his easy manner and to his uncompromising honesty.

Arkady Kirsanov

Arkady, at 23, is a gentle, sympathetic university graduate, drawn to Bazarov's nihilism, but not, ultimately committed to it. Arkady loves his family, thrills to natural beauty, and eventually marries a gentle young woman in the tradition of his fathers. As his sweetheart remarks, Arkady is "tame" and not at all like Bazarov who is a "wild animal" "strong [and] full of force."

At times, as Bazarov's temperamental and philosophical foil, Arkady seems week, ineffectual and silly. He illuminates Bazarov's great commitment and readiness for sacrifice by his own caution and traditionalism. Although we like Arkady for his simplicity and gentleness, he could never hold us for the length of a novel. He is simply not that interesting.

Anna Sergyevna Odintsov (A)

A rich and beautiful widow, Anna is, in ways, the most complicated character in the novel. At 29, she seems already to have exhausted her emotions and possibilities for experience. She was extremely attached to her gambler father, and after his death was thrown into a life of privation and solitude. Her marriage to the repulsive Odintsov taught her the values of hard-headedness over emotional indulgence. Anna's passions were once perhaps as great as Bazarov's but she has learned to suppress all feeling in the interest of comfort, peace of mind and tranquility.

Anna is selfish, powerful and at times overbearing. She is Bazarov's match and perhaps his downfall (having "given" himself to her unsuccessfully, he is forced to recognize the cracks in his own steely armor). Anna represents a class of emancipated intellectuals who, while living within existing traditions, act according to their own convictions and knowledge.

Katya (Katerina Sergyevna)

Anna's 18-year-old sister is as much her foil as Arkady is Bazarov's. She has lived her life under Anna's domination and completely in her shadow. Katya is shy, sweet and gentle. She is intelligent, talented and submissive. Her life with Arkady will be traditional, enlightened and fulfilling.

Nikolai Petrovitch Kirsanov

Nikolai Kirsanov, like his son Arkady, is sweet and gentle and generally ineffectual. When his beloved wife died he poured all his love on his adored son and he now desperately wants to please and communicate with the young man. He is bewildered and cowed by Bazarov's new ideas, and yet eager to understand them so that he may remain a "modern man." Nikolai is filled with humility and tenderness. His love for the young Fenitchka is touching, but his desire to do the right thing in everyone's eyes leaves him weak and uncommitted. Kirsanov is a perfect representative of a generation of intelligent reformers (men of the 40s) who, to their great bewilderment, have been replaced and superannuated by the vehement young generation of radicals (the men of the 60s).

Fenitchka

Fenitchka came to Kirsanov's house as the daughter of his housekeeper. When her mother died, Fenitchka's loneliness, simplicity and youth greatly moved Kirsanov and she became his mistress. If ever a young girl can be innocent while being a mistress and bearing an illegitimate son-Fenitchka is innocent. She is simple, utterly guileless, humble and vulnerable.

Pavel Petrovitch Kirsanov

The old-fashioned, effete aristocracy is caricatured and lambasted in the form of Nikolai's perfumed and manicured elder brother Pavel. Although he lives in the provinces, Pavel affects all the manners of the urban aristocrat. He dresses in the latest dandy fashions, reads only foreign literature, and ineffectually broods over his ruined life (ruined by foolish love). Pavel's mannerisms and pretensions are utterly repelling. Bazarov loathes him and Fenitchka fears him. There is absolutely no place for the handsome "relic" of the old days in Russia of the 1860s. We might sympathize with his bitter and frustrated life but, along with Turgenev, we must judge him to be a "dead man."

Vassily Ivanovitch Bazarov

Unlike Pavel, Bazarov's old father, although a member of a past generation, excites not our contempt but our love and tenderness. A fussy, verbose old man, hopelessly behind the times, at least he is not a posturing aristocrat. His life is governed by love, consideration and desire to please. Although the "new Russia" may need to rid itself of its old Bazarovs in matters of philosophy and technique, it will never endure without his human qualities of tenderness and self-sacrifice.

Arina Vlasyevna Bazarov (A)

Bazarov's mother makes no attempt to "keep up" with her son. She neither pretends nor desires to understand his ideas. She is religious, superstitious and excessively emotional. She is the old Russian mother, concerned with food and comfort and devotion. She fears her son utterly and mourns his death inconsolably.

Victor Sitnikov

Bazarov's self-proclaimed disciple is a devastating caricature of the "emancipated" Slavophile (see Introduction). He talks too much about nothing and has no comprehension of the undigested ideas he spouts. He is the cringing fool of the sort which parasitically attaches himself to strong thinkers and leaders.

FATHERS AND SONS

CRITICAL COMMENTARY

TURGENEV

Turgenev himself wrote an essay on *Fathers and Sons* which is included in his "Literary Reminiscences." Written in 1868-69, while the author was in Baden-Baden, the article tells of Turgenev's inspiration for Bazarov and of his intentions while creating him. Inspired by a young Russian doctor he had met, Turgenev tried to show in Bazarov something of what he saw going on around him in the young generation. But he feared, since the phenomena were recorded nowhere else, that he was "chasing after a phantom."

Bazarov expresses himself in "harsh and unceremonious tones" because Turgenev was merely recording what he had seen, not making up a character: " 'Life happened to be like that' my experience told me." Turgenev realizes that some conservative forces took the word "nihilist" and applied it vindictively to the young generation in order to stem their radicalism. "But I never used that word as a pejorative term or with any offensive aim," Turgenev insisted. It is "an exact and appropriate expression of … an historic fact that has made its appearance among us."

HENRY JAMES

He was one of Turgenev's earliest and most ardent admirers. In an essay called "Turgenev and Tolstoy," James discusses Turgenev's great popularity in Europe: "There is perhaps no novelist of alien race who more naturally than Ivan Turgenev inherits a niche in a library for English readers." James is primarily concerned, however, with Turgenev's exquisite and precise melding of form and content. Turgenev, he says, brings "home to us the happy truth of the unity, in a generous talent, of material and form-of their being inevitable faces of the same medal."

The material to which Turgenev weds his form is the familiar stuff of life, "the world of character and feeling, the world of relations ... his air is that of the great central region of passion and motive, of the usual, the inevitable, the ultimate." In realizing the familiar, Turgenev had first to realize the character and this he did with no contrivances. "No one has had a closer vision, or a hand at once more ironic and more tender, for the individual figure."

James admires in Turgenev the ability to make his characters live through "the finest and tenderest touches." He is, James insists, "the novelist's novelist."

J. A. T. LLOYD

In his literary biography of Turgenev, Lloyd discusses *Fathers and Sons* as a social document. Bazarov is the "heroic rebel" who interprets in action "the challenge of freedom coherently, scientifically, from the head ... rather than from the heart." In Bazarov's death, Lloyd finds that "the sluggish ignorance of the old Russia has beaten the innovator.... He had wished to conquer the background of Russia, but it was this very background that was to consume and absorb him." Bazarov, according to Lloyd, had stood for a new generation, for "a new race of Russians." And he had been beaten by inertia: "His voice had never been heard." Lloyd sees in Bazarov's death an indictment of Russia and a glorification of the young nihilist.

EDMUND WILSON

The famous modern critic, in an essay entitled "Turgenev and the Life-Giving Drop" details the gruesome conflicts of Turgenev's childhood and his continuing humiliations by his despotic mother. Wilson shows how Turgenev's relationships with his mother, and later with Pauline Viardot, are reflected over and over in the writer's choice of themes. "The content of Ivan's early work is mostly in one way or another a product of his mother's personality." While his mother was still alive, Turgenev wrote persistently of an irresistible force of evil which always appeared in a masculine form. After she died he wrote frequently of the destructive cold, ruthless, domineering woman.

Turgenev's enduring pessimism "show[s] the permanent stamp of an oppressive, a completely hopeless and a permanently harrowing experience ... Spasskoye for Turgenev was a block of his past; he had grown up in it, been maimed by it, escaped from it."

As for Turgenev's insight into character, Wilson comments: "He is the expert detached observer rather than the searching psychologist." He is most satisfactory "when he is telling you merely what [his characters] say and do, how they look and what one feels about them." Turgenev's "particular forte," points out Wilson in agreement with Henry James, is dramatizing "what people show themselves to be in relation to other people."

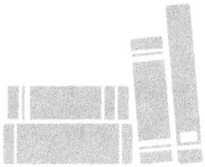

FATHERS AND SONS

ESSAY QUESTIONS AND ANSWERS

Question: After *Fathers and Sons* was published the young reformers berated Turgenev for denigrating one of their numbers. Why did they think the author was contemptuous of Bazarov?

Answer: In his manners and appearance Bazarov is brash, crass, rude and inconsiderate. He speaks harshly to everyone who disagrees with him and respects no person or idea. He is inconsiderate of friends, relatives and "disciples" alike and seems to think of no one but himself and of nothing but his own "philosophy." Bazarov, an incredible egotist, has neither patience nor tolerance for human weakness and foible. He is selfish and presumptuous.

But worse than all this, Bazarov dies without accomplishing a thing. He is, ultimately, no more effective than the "fathers" he so deplores. All his theorizing and venom lead to nothing-he dies from a careless mistake, not a heroic sacrifice. He has made much noise, but by his early death the noise seems more sound than substance. He dies unfulfilled, unaccomplished and unmourned by any but his doting parents.

Question: Turgenev protested that far from criticizing Bazarov he expected the nihilist to win sympathy for the young progressives. What evidence do we have of that intention?

Answer: Bazarov is the only truly vital character in the novel. His fierce dedication to ideas and his willingness to sacrifice for ideals compel admiration and respect. His manner may be rough but his dedication and intensity are so unusual and consuming that we feel exceptions may be made for his rudeness.

For all his fervent devotion to the future, Bazarov is far from inhuman in the present. He has a ready and ironic wit and occasional devastating insights into his own unimportance. Despite his great efforts at objectivity and detachment he falls madly, passionately, hopelessly in love. In his love he is "human" with a vengeance and vulnerable like any other man.

As for his short, unproductive life, the burden falls on Russia not on Bazarov. In death, Bazarov is magnificent. He shows no fear, fights desperately for his dignity and faces his painful dying with utmost bravery. It is Russia's failing that Bazarov died ineffective. Her effete aristocrats, ineffectual middle classes and drunken, oppressed peasantry were not yet ready for - him for his ideas or his zeal. Bazarov was, simply, born too early for his backward country. Had Russia's doctors been abreast of medical progress, he might have recovered and lived till a more receptive time. But as Russia was backward in slavery, farming, education and philosophy, so she was backward in medicine - and the brave, active nihilist was killed by her lethargy and ignorance.

Question: *Fathers and Sons*, like all great literature, is about people. Secondarily, it gives a picture of the social structure of Russia in the 1860s. What classes of people do we see?

Answer: Servants: Emancipation in Russia came in 1861; thus, at the time of the novel (1859) there was still a large servant class. We see two kinds of slaves: the old-fashioned "family retainer" type (Prokofitch at Kirsanov's, Timofeitch at Bazarov's) grateful for their acceptance and security in the household, and the younger, brazen and insolent men of the future (Piotr at Kirsanov's) who affect foppish airs and sniff their freedom in the wind.

Peasants: Most of Russia's population in 1859 belonged to the peasantry. It was their freedom which the young reformers so zealously sought. But the peasants, as we see them at Kirsanov's, are a distasteful lot, corrupted by their centuries of oppression. They are drunken, thieving, grasping, dishonest and completely ignorant. They would rather break a machine than run it, rather go off on a binge than cultivate their land.

Old generation-poor: In the old Bazarovs we see a class of unsuccessful, unenlightened conservatives. Their minds grown rusty, they live by emotion and superstition, not knowledge and enlightenment. They are gentle and loving and totally ineffective in a land which must meet the future by revolution.

Old generation-rich: While the poor Bazarovs are pathetic and useless, the aristocratic Pavel is despicable and destructive. He aggressively clings to his outdated aristocracy, scorning the land and those who work it. He furiously resists the erosion of European-type autocracy, and he will not sully his manicured hands whether or not the future of his country demands it. Nikolai, on the other hand, has tried desperately, though hopelessly, to look toward the future. He has already freed his peasants and introduced new methods and machinery. He is enlightened within his limited potential, but simply lacks the energy, organization and authority to make a "go" of the new life. His farm fails beneath him as he bungles its management with the very best of intentions.

Government Officials: The most scathing caricatures are reserved for self-inflated officials and pseudo-emancipes (see below). Matvy Ilyitch, the unctuous petty official, is ridiculous and despicable. He overevaluates his own importance and has neither the intelligence nor wit to do more than seem "grand" at a provincial ball. The foolish provincial Governor, for his part, is as unable to organize his breakfast as his duties-he is nothing more or less than an incompetent fool.

Pseudo-Emancipes: If Turgenev laughs at the officials, he contemptuously derides the empty liberals. Both the unkempt Mme. Kukshin and the simpering Slavophile, Sitnikov, are more destructive of genuine, thoughtful progress than are the members of the uncomprehending old generation.

Reformers: We see three representatives of the young generation of reformers: Arkady, liberal and fully in sympathy with the revolutionary wave, lacks the energy and strength to do more than tag along after it. Anna Sergyevna, who is intelligent, up-to-date and passionate, clings to her own status quo rather than rock her peaceful boat. Bazarov devotes his soul and life to modernizing the country.

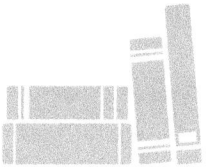

FATHERS AND SONS

BIBLIOGRAPHY

Because Turgenev is so polished and refined a writer, the reader of translations loses a great deal of the author's original and unique style. Unfortunately, few translations of *Fathers and Sons* capture at once Turgenev's sense, style and taut language. A few texts are listed below from which the reader can make his choice.

Turgenev, Ivan, *Fathers and Sons*, translated by Constance Garnett, introduction by Herbert J. Muller (New York, 1950). The standard, but barely adequate, translation by Constance Garnett, with a thorough, practical introduction.

____, *Fathers and Sons*, translated by Constance Garnett, edited and revised by Lucy M. Cores (New York, 1942). Lucy Cores updates. Constance Garnett's translation and presents a sympathetic and anecdotal introduction to the novel.

____, *Fathers and Children*, translated by Richard Hare (New York, 1960). Hare's translation (in paperback) is clear, modern and highly readable although it fails to capture fully Turgenev's delicate style.

____, *Fathers and Children*, translated by Avril Pyman, introduction by Nikola y Andreyev (London, 1962). Miss Pyman offers a translation which conveys elegance without distracting from strength. She avoids "modernisms" and adheres as closely as possible to Turgenev's style. To avoid confusion Miss Pyman includes useful footnotes when the Russian term or concept is alien to English readers.

Letters, Etc.

Lehrman, Edgar H., *Turgenev's Letters*, A Selection (New York, 1961). Mr. Lehrman has collected and translated an interesting and valuable selection of Russian, French and German letters. In several of them Turgenev discusses his feelings about Bazarov.

Turgenev, Ivan, "Literary Reminiscences," translated by David Magarshack, essay by Edmund Wilson (New York, 1958). Wilson's essay is a brilliant, psychologically oriented study of Turgenev's themes. One of the "reminiscences" is an article by Turgenev written in 1868-69, entitled "Apropos of *Fathers and Sons*." It is crucial to the understanding of the author's intentions in writing the novel.

Biographies

Lloyd, J. A. T., *Ivan Turgenev* (London, 1942). Lloyd traces the relationship between Turgenev's life and works, showing how the novelist put much autobiography into his writings.

Magarshack, David, *Turgenev, A Life* (New York, 1954). A thorough and detailed biography by this famous scholar of Russian literature.

Yarmolinsky, Avrahm, *Turgenev, The Man, His Art and His Age* (New York, 1926). This early study (in English) of Turgenev's life and times provides insightful and full background material for an intelligent appraisal of the author's work.

Zhitova, Varvara, *The Turgenev Family* (New York, 1947). Published first in Russia in 1884, this biography by Turgenev's step-sister (adopted at birth by Turgenev's mother) tells of the havoc the novelist's mother created around her.

Criticism

Freeborn, Richard, *Turgenev: The Novelist's Novelist* (London, 1960). Freeborn, with great admiration, traces Turgenev's literary development, and thoroughly analyzes structure and style.

Hirschkowitz, Harry, *Democratic Ideas in Turgenev's Novels* (New York, 1932). As the title indicates, the critic traces Turgenev's "philosophy" in his novels, showing his unvarying desire for enlightenment and democracy.

Slonim, Marc, *The **Epic** of Russian Literature* (New York, 1950). The first volume of this impressive work deals with Russian literature "from its origins through Tolstoy." The second part deals with the period from the 1870s to the present. Twenty-five years of research and study went into this comprehensive, brilliant analysis of Russian literature. Mr. Slonim includes a lengthy section on Turgenev.

James, Henry, *The Future of the Novel* (New York, 1956). This is a book of collected essays by James. The essay entitled "Turgenev and Tolstoy," written in 1897, shows James' great admiration for Turgenev's meshing of form and content, and for his economy of style.

Bibliography

Gettman, R. A., *Turgenev in England and America* (Urbana, 1941). A partial, but highly useful bibliography of works and criticism in English, which, however, is now 25 years out of date.

www.ingramcontent.com/pod-product-compliance
Lightning Source LLC
LaVergne TN
LVHW011727060526
838200LV00051B/3059